"As a woman who has gone thro ___ know how lonely the journey car ___ huge difference: hope for your he ___ ...iend to walk with you. Jennifer Kostick offers both on these pages as she shares her personal story as well as much-needed encouragement."

Holley Gerth, best-selling author of
You're Going to Be Okay

"Jennifer's story is so powerful! Readers will find her honesty, transparency, and vulnerability deeply moving, her faith encouraging, and her hope truly inspiring!"

Christin Ditchfield, author of
What Women Should Know About Facing Fear

"I'm always amazed by the powerful stories women share related to fertility and faith. Each journey, a trial by fire that produces a God-breathed warrior spirit. Jennifer Kosticks' battle, and subsequent victory, is infused with the miraculous power of God. I cried, I cheered, I prayed. And I believed. Written with authenticity and heart, Jennifer shares the wisdom of a veteran, the soul of a girl....who won't give up on God. Any woman, walking through a similar journey would be challenged and inspired to give Him a try."

Lisha Epperson, seespeakhearmama.com

"Nothing to Hold but Hope is a coffee date for the soul. Reading Jennifer's story of pain and redemption is like sitting down with a dear friend or mentor, and allowing your heart to be ministered to by someone you love and trust. Any woman who has journeyed down the painful road of infertility, miscarriage, or stillbirth will find that Jennifer's story resonates within her, and will find hope and encouragement in knowing she is not alone in her grief, fear, and struggle, and she will recognize the challenge to relinquish her fear and anger to the Peace Giver."

"Jennifer shares her story with frankness and humility, and offers readers comfort and hope to hold on to."

Amanda Erickson, aroyaldaughter.com

Nothing to Hold but Hope

Nothing to Hold but Hope:

One woman's journey through

miscarriage,

stillbirth, and infertility

Jennifer Kostick

Contents

I dedicate this book to the memory of my beautiful grandmother, Jane. She was a gift straight from Jesus and the most humble human being I have ever known. I'm not sure if she ever recognized how holy her work was in my life. She lived and died giving everything she had to her family. Her hands in my life were the hands of God working through her. To Him be the Glory! I know you're holding my babies tight, grandma. I love you bushels and bushels full! Until we meet again...

Introduction

I love to read! When I finish a good book, I am always amazed by the time and talent poured into it by the author. The research required to write a novel leads authors all over the world to interview interesting people, landscape a story, and bring it to life.

The story I have to tell wasn't preplanned in the recesses of my mind, just waiting for me to capture it with pen and paper. There are no exotic places for your mind's eye to visualize. Instead, it is a dose of reality that shaped who I am today. I was forced to take a good, hard look in the mirror and recognize what I did and did not like about myself. I found that you can't run from your problems, because wherever you go, they are there with you. My journey left me with scars on my heart, but what I gained spiritually from it was worth every tear that was shed.

Like most authors, I did my research, but only because I lived every detail. I breathed it in and out. The idea that "everyone has a story" has become cliché, but it's true. Through our pain God is setting out to accomplish something beautiful within us, and how we handle struggle helps determine who we are. Each of our stories is carefully orchestrated by the Creator, but, unlike the conductor of an orchestra, who directs the instruments' ebb and flow of music, our God leaves the choice of proper dynamics to us.

He gives us exactly what we need along the way, but because He also gives us free will, we have to be willing to accept and use it. We are all a work in progress, and we will be until the day we find ourselves before His throne.

The chapter of my story you're about to learn is just one piece of the puzzle that makes me who I am. I pray that these fifteen years of my life will give you strength if you or someone you love is in the midst of a similar journey.

Since you are reading this, chances are that you have experienced miscarriage, stillbirth, or infertility. I know the pain of all three, and I understand the sense of hopelessness that tears at the heart. I want to share my struggles with you, for you. My prayer is that through my testimony, you will regain hope and find your strength in Him.

A woman who lost a baby during childbirth once asked me, "How did you do it? How did you get through it?" My answer was the same then as it is now: one breath at a time, one day at a time, and, most importantly, one prayer at a time. It was an uphill battle, a tug of war between my will and God's will that became a daily fight for my spiritual survival.

For years, grief served as my unwanted best friend. I barely remembered how to function without it. I knew that Jesus died to take away my pain, but I couldn't rid myself of this antagonistic companion. While I suffered loss after loss with seemingly no end in sight, grief stood by me every step of the way. Anyone who has had multiple losses and has found solace in Christ understands that it takes time to find your footing again. The miraculous part is that we can stand together and recognize that "all things work together for good for those who love Him, and are called according to His purpose" (Romans 8:28, New King James Version).

I don't know who I would be today if not for these hardships, and, frankly, I don't want to know. Honestly, I would not change a thing. I am who I am in Christ because of the trials I have endured. I have come out of the dark, gray clouds into the sun. It takes the love of a Savior who understands pain and knows us better than anyone else ever could to fill us up and make us whole again.

"You are My witnesses," says the Lord,
"and My servant whom I have chosen,
That you may know and believe Me, and
understand that I am He. Before Me there
was no God formed, nor shall there be
after Me." (Isaiah 43:10)

This verse gives me two lifelines:
1. I need to know Him. A personal relationship with Christ will sustain me through difficult times.

2. I have to believe Him! This is imperative. If I truly believe His word, then I am able to rest knowing that He alone is in control.

It took me a long time to grasp the principle of this verse. I battled my own need to "fix" my situation. I was one big ball of stress trying to make sense of it all. Of all the emotions I faced, my desire for control was probably the most detrimental. It was not until I neared the end of my battle that the following scripture took root.

> The end of a thing is better than its beginning; the patient in spirit is better than the proud in spirit. (Ecclesiastes 7:8)

I imagine our lives as giant picture windows. Only bits and pieces of what is on the other side of the window are visible. Over time, we see and understand more of why we are where we are – and of what God intends for us. If we knew God's perfect ending, we could endure waiting for more of the picture to be revealed. But since we don't know that ending, and we can't see the whole work of the Creator at once, we need to exercise patience and push away our need to control events.

We need to trust in the One who knows all and who is All. If we follow what He has for us, then the end certainly will be better than the beginning. There is no room for our pride. We don't have the ability to take over the work of the Artist. It is impossible to finish the picture the way we see fit.

I often wanted to take over the driver's seat of my life, deciding which way to turn and how fast to travel. When I finally understood that I needed to give up my illusion of control (and that I actually had none in the first place), I opened myself up to a brand new dimension of what God had for me. This opened up my heart and soul for a miraculous healing. By "miraculous," I don't mean that healing took place in an instant. Sometimes we experience miracles one step at a time.

In 1997, my husband, brother-in-law, and two other family members were in a car accident caused by a drunk driver. My brother-in-law Levi sustained brain damage. The doctors gave little hope, and while he spent weeks in a coma, everyone prayed for a miracle. With all my heart I believed that when he awoke from his coma that he would just be "Levi" again, and that there would be no long-term effects. After all, that's the way it happens in the movies: the main character wakes from a coma that he has been in for years and speaks with such fluency that it appears as if he was just taking a power nap. But it's not like the movies at all. For months, Levi relearned to walk, talk, and even read. Every time he accomplished a minor goal, like speaking in full sentences, we experienced a miracle. It did not happen overnight, but it happened just the same.

A healing of the heart can be much like waking out of a coma. It is a process. Your thought patterns can shift. You may feel emotionally unstable. Your personality may seem to have changed completely. You may feel that, in the midst of suffering, you have lost yourself. Still, every time you have enough faith to press into God, you unlock hope. My experience taught me that you cannot walk the tight rope of soul-killing emotion without hope. If today is the day that you decide to press into God, then today you might experience a miracle without even realizing it.

Those of us who have a personal relationship with Jesus sometimes make it harder to go through trials in life because we want a reason why. After all, we are "good people," and we serve the Lord. In case you are not already aware, allow me to shine a little light on this subject: bad things happen to "good," godly people. That's just the way it is. So many times I asked the Lord, "What is the reason for all this?" I don't think I ever received a clear answer, but deep down in my heart, I know that I did not suffer all those years for nothing.

I am humbled that you have already taken the time to open up this book and read about my journey. I hope to show you a glimmer of light in a dark place and lighten the load of your burden by sharing what helped me. I hope that, because of my transparency, you will see the mistakes I made along the way and how to avoid them. Maybe you'll simply recognize that you are not alone.

I might not say anything new to you – not after all the advice you've already heard. I am not a medical professional. I do not claim to be able to grace you with some amount of wonderful wisdom. I just want to help you.

From a physical standpoint, the situation that you are enduring is unique to you. Each body is unique, and your medical diagnosis may be different from the one that I had. What is the same is the sense of loss – not just the loss you feel from coping with miscarriage or stillbirth, but also the loss from being unable to become pregnant. Infertility creates a race against the clock, causing you to ruminate over all the time you feel you lost.

Because you are working overtime to process your thoughts and emotions, you might think that the answer to your problem is to have a baby. God might be doing something else in the inner workings of your heart. The answer to complex equations in our lives, especially those brought by infertility, miscarriage, or stillbirth, cannot be worked out without faith, because the variables are always changing.

The road is tough, but healing your heart takes readiness. Are you ready to hear what God is speaking to you? Is your heart open to it? The keys to helping your broken heart heal all depend upon whether you are ready to know and believe Christ.

The intent of this book is simply to share my testimony with you. I want you to realize you are not alone. If you are in the midst of a battle with infertility, or if you have dealt with a loss and are now pregnant again, you may find yourself facing a daily fear of the outcome of your circumstance. Regardless of the specifics of your battle, my prayer for you remains the same. I pray for hope, peace, and strength to fill you, as well as unshakeable reliance on God.

1

A Little Background

I always wanted to be a wife and mother. These aspirations may seem very 1950s, but creating a happy nuclear family – with two parents who do not just love each other but are in love with each other – was the only thing I really wanted in life.

I grant that some of this probably came from the fact I come from a divorced family, and even though I do not consider my siblings to be "half" siblings, the biological facts are that with one brother I share a mother, and with the other a father, which plainly means that is what we are – half siblings. Having a husband who loved me and having children with him alone was always a dream of mine.

When I was around the age of ten, I went to a harvest party on Halloween night at a local church. As part of the festivities, the adult leaders were asking some of the children questions. They asked me, "If you could be any person from the Bible, who would you be and why?" My answer came quickly: "I would want to be Mary, because she is the mother of Jesus."

....

I am sharing this tiny, seemingly insignificant part of my childhood with you because, for as long as I can remember, I felt a deep desire to be a mother. I have no idea why the memory of that moment at that party has stayed with me so vividly, but it does help me illustrate a picture of my heart to you.

I count myself extremely blessed to have grown up attending a private Christian school. It was – and still is – a very small school without a lot of material things to offer but with an undeniable wealth of spiritual knowledge. I met my husband Paul at that school as a young teenager. We were high school sweethearts. We dreamed about marriage from the time I was fifteen and he was sixteen. In June of 1990, Paul graduated from high school, and he asked me to marry him. I am a year younger than he, so I was engaged my senior year. While my friends were choosing colleges, I was planning a wedding. We married in August of 1991, at the very young ages of eighteen and nineteen.

Marrying young and having a healthy marriage is a rarity, especially when dealing with the trials and tribulations that come with this life. Either people stick together and become closer, or they run as far and as fast from each other as they can. My husband and I have just recently celebrated our twenty-second wedding anniversary. We are closer than ever. We have endured great trials, and in this area of our lives, we have finally claimed victory!

2

First Pregnancy

When Paul and I were first married, I worked at a day care center. He was both working and attending college at the time. Still so young, we struggled financially, and it seemed that a job working with children would be perfect for me. I fell completely in love with the children. Working with them every day caused me to want to have a child of my own. After talking with my husband, I decided to quit the birth control pill. Looking back, it's hard to believe it was so easy. Within three months, I was pregnant. I didn't have to worry about details like timing or graphing my temperature. I didn't even know how to calculate all those things at that point in my life. I wanted to be pregnant, and I was. Wow, what a blessing! Naïveté truly can be pure bliss.

My pregnancy was for the most part normal, for the baby at least. I had no bleeding or worry of having any bleeding due to my young, this-is-all-going-to-work-out-perfectly mind set. However, I was very sick! The way my body dealt with morning sickness redefined the term. I threw up for months on end, lost weight before I gained any, and lost much of my strength in the process. The medical term for this is hyper emesis gravid arum. This is a very difficult condition for any woman to tolerate, let alone a nineteen-year-old with a new, young, handsome husband who was reduced to cleaning up my vomit night and day because I was too weak to do it myself.

We laugh today about how broke we were, and about how he would spend his last thirty dollars taking me out to eat. The problem was that I would immediately throw up his entire thirty dollars' worth of food in the parking lot promptly after leaving the restaurant. There was not one establishment I visited on a regular basis where I didn't end up sick, at least once. Oh, and did I mention I became ill with chicken pox in the first trimester? Yes, I did!

The risk of contracting chicken pox early in a pregnancy is congenital varicella syndrome. The most common manifestation of congenital varicella syndrome is scarring of the baby's skin. However, other abnormalities that can occur include a smaller than normal head, eye problems, low birth weight, small limbs, and mental handicap (CDC). Thankfully, we didn't encounter any of these anomalies. I gave birth to a healthy baby boy on December 3, 1992. Today he is twenty-one years old and the joy of my life. God used those beautiful blue eyes of that precious baby boy to help me through many dark days ahead.

Some of us try for what seems forever to become pregnant; others can never experience pregnancy at all. Some conceive as soon as they decide it is time, and some even have what we refer to as "accidents." I experienced almost all of these situations. I went through years of infertility, and I became pregnant when I decided I wanted to be pregnant. I even once had an unexpected, "accidental" pregnancy.

I now realize these little "accidents," as so many people fondly refer to them, are the most beautiful treasured gifts straight from heaven – if you are blessed enough to keep them. Later, after years of grieving, I learned that they are also a blessing, even if you are unable to keep them. This brings me to my second pregnancy.

3

Second Pregnancy

When my son was seven months old, I discovered that I was pregnant again. This was my one and only "accident." I remember physically feeling fine, but missing my period. In those days I had very regular periods, so this was a tip off that something was going on.

It was now July of 1993. Our son Pauly was doing all the adorable little things that babies of that age do. We were overjoyed with him. I was not working anymore. Because I had become so sick during my pregnancy with Pauly, I had to quit my job. My husband was still working and going to school.

Even though we struggled financially and my husband was so busy, I have a smile on my face right now as I think about what a joyful and simple time it was. We hadn't really had any of life's disturbances to cloud our vision and bring us down – not yet.

When the pregnancy test result read positive, I was so excited. I knew that, financially, things would be more difficult, but none of that mattered to me or Paul. We were going to have a new baby! A sibling for our son! I was a step closer to accomplishing my dream of having the family I had always desired.

The day I learned I was pregnant was the same day I happened to be leaving on a cross country road trip. My in-laws were moving from Pennsylvania, where we all lived, to California. My mother-in-law asked me to drive with her cross country and stay for a couple of weeks. We were only there a few days when I started to have some spotting.

At first, I just kept telling myself that the spotting meant nothing, and that it would go away. It didn't. It wasn't long until the spotting turned to heavier bleeding much like a period.

When I returned home to Pennsylvania a couple days later, I called my doctor. The bleeding had slowed to a spotting by then, but after an examination the doctor determined that I needed a D&C.

A dilatation and curettage is a surgical procedure done during a first trimester miscarriage. Dilatation means to open up, and curettage means to clean out the contents of the uterus.

This was a simple procedure, and I was assured by the doctor that miscarriage is very common, and I should not worry.

I remember feeling, for lack of a better description, dazed by the miscarriage. Deep down I knew something wasn't right. I was not sick like I had been from the beginning of my previous pregnancy, but I had rationalized this, because all pregnancies are different. When all was said and done, I felt a pang of loneliness coming from somewhere deep within me

I dealt with an amazing amount of loss in my pursuit

....

of another child. Still, I will say this: it does not matter if you have had one miscarriage or one hundred. This kind of loss is difficult. It feels as if you were robbed, except that what you lost can never be replaced. Another child will not fill the void the other little life left behind. If you have had many losses, it is important that you still feel for the woman that has "only" suffered one loss and has the ability to become pregnant again whenever she wants. Do not grow callous. Do not look for company in your own misery. After all, that word *only* a few sentences ago can be hurtful and misrepresenting. One loss is one too many. It can devastate your being and disrupt the certainty you felt in life.

4

Strongholds

As I share my story, what comes to mind is the tree of the knowledge of good and evil in the biblical book of Genesis. Adam and Eve's eyes were opened after they ate from the tree. When we are young, we seem to live in our own private Garden of Eden, feeling invincible and strong. The older we become, after taking a nice big bite of the realities we experience in life, the feeling of invincibility we once had is snatched from us. We then become more aware of our fears, and fears can become strongholds.

To this day, I recall exactly where I was when that fear developed in me. I was talking with a group of women when someone shared her story about having a miscarriage. In that moment I realized, This could happen to me. I can't be sure why I was instantaneously gripped by that new fear, but my spirit tells me I had a weakness in that area that I wasn't aware of at the time, and Satan honed in on it and attacked.

I want to make sure not to give credit to the enemy where it is not due. Sometimes we tend to pollute our own minds with fear, doubt, and unbelief, making us easy targets for strongholds to develop. We need to keep in mind that

....

when we accept Christ as our Savior, we are covered with the blood that He shed when He died for us. We only need to give our fears to Him in order to be delivered of them, yet this concept seems to take a lifetime to conquer. It's much easier said than done.

I needed to grasp onto God and give Him my fear, but I was not as spiritually mature as I needed to be to fight it. I was a Christian, went to church, and lived for God. Still, my prayer life was not what it should have been, and I wasn't reading the Bible the way I should have. Make no mistake; I don't mean to convey that this miscarriage (or any other negative thing) happened because I wasn't pressing into God enough. I believe it was simply part of His will for me. Proverbs 3:5 says it best: "Trust in the Lord with all your heart, and lean not on your own understanding." Things like this are not always meant for us to understand.

Save, Lord! May the King answer us when we call. (Psalm 20:9)

My husband and I spend a lot of time ministering to teenagers. We started a youth ministry at our church several years ago, and it has been a true blessing. However, trying to help young adults understand why God answers some prayers the way we want them answered – and not other prayers – can be a long uphill climb. When teens are hurting and it seems as if God does not heed their prayers, we can find it difficult to explain. We have watched as our young adults deal with sick parents, sibling deaths, and hard battles with self image. We have seen teens suffer everything from breakups to not being hired for a job they want and not being accepted into their college of choice.

Because these issues are so important to them, young people sometimes weigh how much God loves them based on whether He answers their prayers the way they want. And guess what? Most adults are not much different, especially when we are begging God for something as important and life changing as having a child.

I believe with my whole heart that God cares about every issue that we care about, no matter how big or small. I also believe that if our wants and needs are not part of His plan, then it is not what is best for us and God might say, "No," or "Not now." God will answer in His own way, in His own time. It does not mean He doesn't love us. It means that He loves us too much for the answer to be any less than what He has designed it to be. Our job is to keep praying, trusting, and believing that the King will answer when we call.

A more intimate prayer life and more time in His Word on a regular basis would have equipped me to fight the battles in my life. I've learned that when I dig deep in His word, my focus shifts from my own bleak problems to His amazing majesty. It is in my moments alone with Him that I recognize how small I am and how big He is.

When I am weak, He is strong. He gives us His strength to fight. As things turned out, I had quite a fight ahead of me.

5

Third Pregnancy

Because my second pregnancy was not planned, we waited a while to become pregnant again. About a year later, in 1994, the time seemed right. As before, conception was easy, and we were thrilled to see a positive pregnancy test.

About eight weeks into the pregnancy, I had a routine doctor's appointment, where the doctor performed an early ultrasound. Sadly, he discovered the baby had no heartbeat and the sac was not intact.

Soon afterward, the spotting started. We did some follow up blood work which confirmed the loss of the pregnancy, and the doctor decided to schedule a D&C. I was left heartbroken and confused. I had no idea why something like this would happen to me twice in a row.

I was so young at the time, and I had many misconceptions about miscarriage. I could not wrap my brain around the fact that someone my age could experience back-to-back miscarriages. After all, didn't you have to be older for that to happen?

After this, more fear began to set in. Would I ever have another child? Was there something more seriously wrong with me that the doctors were unaware of? Questions without answers left me completely overwhelmed, and fear dug deeper and deeper into my soul.

I've always had a weakness where fear is concerned. I've wrestled with it as long as I can remember. For example, I used to be afraid of elevators. As a small child, I belonged to a church group called pioneer girls, and once, we went on a field trip to the Cathedral of Learning at the University of Pittsburgh. We were to tour the entire building: all forty-two stories. I panicked in the elevator and made the whole troop and all the leaders walk the stairs all the way to the top, because I was afraid! Today, I can look back at that day and laugh.

However, my fear affected much more than my being responsible for a group of girls getting some extra exercise. It also deprived me of seeing my grandfather for the last time. He was in the hospital suffering from cancer. My mother asked if I wanted to go see him, warning that taking an elevator would be necessary. I was eight years old at the time and did not understand the possible ramifications of not visiting him. I opted not to go because of my fear of elevators. He died not long afterward from the cancer.

Fear is a lot like cancer; it eats away at you and steals your joy. John 10:10 states, "The thief does not come except to steal, and to kill, and to destroy. I have come that they may have life, and that they may have it more abundantly." The first part of this verse speaks of what the enemy has come to do, but we need to keep our thoughts focused even more on the second part of the verse. We can never forget why Jesus came – that we may have life and have it more abundantly! We cannot hold onto an abundant life or even the hope of an abundant life when imprisoned by fear.

> Thus says the Lord: "Stand in the ways
> and see, and ask for the old paths, where
> the good way is, and walk in it; then you
> will find rest for your souls." But they said,
> "We will not walk in it." (Jeremiah 6:16)

These words that God spoke in the days of Jeremiah are just as relevant today. Following "old paths" refers to following the ways of our godly predecessors. We need to follow old paths to find rest.

King David, as well as many of the Bible's heroes, had days of feeling despondent and fear-filled, yet he chose to walk in the "old paths" – paths paved with faith and obedience. I had to learn – and I'm still learning – to fracture fear in my life.

To fracture something is a process. It is hard to make a clean break from fear, because we all revisit it on a regular basis. For me it is a process of tearing away the layers of fear to complete the fracture. In breaking through the fear, I find myself walking closer with my God on the "old path."

As for my fear with the second miscarriage, my doctor thought it was just a "fluke" and told me not to worry. We followed the doctor's advice to wait a little while and allow my body to recover before trying again. Three months later we decided it was time.

6

Fourth Pregnancy

The next time we tried for a baby, it took six months. At the time, six months seemed like an eternity. As I hit the rewind button in my mind and remember all the emotions I felt, it seems laughable to have thought that those six months were a long time to wait for anything. For most healthy couples, it is considered completely normal to take up to a year to become pregnant.

When I learned I was pregnant, I was elated but apprehensive, considering my two previous losses. By the time I was six weeks into the pregnancy, I was vomiting on a regular basis, a telltale sign that all was well. I was never sick with the two pregnancies that ended in miscarriage, so I took comfort thinking that the sicker I was, the healthier the pregnancy was. I was praising God every time I was over the toilet puking my guts out, because I knew this baby was okay! At twelve weeks into the pregnancy we heard a healthy heartbeat. I breathed a sigh of relief.

This was a time of new beginnings, some welcome and some not. We had moved to California two months prior to this pregnancy. I now had a new obstetrician. She is a wonderful Christian woman and an amazing doctor whom God placed in my life for a specific purpose.

I hadn't made any new friends, though, and all of my family was in Pennsylvania. It helped that my husband's family lived close to us, but most of the time, all these new beginnings brought fresh tears. I was hyperemotional from the pregnancy. I missed my family and friends, and my husband was working very long hours. Most of my days felt never-ending. My son was almost three at the time, and, as every stay-at-home mother of a young child knows, it was wonderful and challenging all at the same time. Time alone was rare and the longing for adult conversation was the norm.

My life was different from anything I had ever known. Everywhere I went there were new faces, and I should add that I ended up lost everywhere I went. I needed a map to go to the grocery store. There were days when all these "new adventures" overwhelmed me. But, as days turned into weeks and weeks into months, I was making my way in a new world. I had a husband with whom I was in love, a son who brought me joy, and a new baby on the way. During this time I recorded the events of my life in a prayer journal. Most of the prayers in the journal were prayers of thanksgiving for my son and new, beautiful baby growing inside me.

In my fifth month, I had an ultrasound. The results were excellent. We were having a healthy baby! The doctor also told us there was an eighty percent chance the baby was a girl! I knew in my heart she was a girl from the beginning. We named her Courtney Elizabeth.

We were living in an apartment at the time, and because of limited storage space, I decided to hold off buying anything for her until the end of my pregnancy. In the end, this proved to be a huge blessing, but anyone who knows me also knows this was a miraculous feat! Patience is not my virtue, especially when it comes to shopping! But God is so good. He shows up in every detail of every situation without fail.

Things proceeded fantastically. Time flew by, and the next thing I knew, I was thirty-four weeks into my pregnancy and making bets with my husband on whether this baby would be early or late. I had started purchasing minimal things (I couldn't completely wait until the end): a few dresses and headbands that I just could not resist buying.

On the morning of Monday, July 1, 1996, I woke up not feeling right. The day before, I had noticed a great deal of swelling in my ankles, and even though the swelling was down, something just seemed "off." I slowly realized that I had not felt the baby move since the day before.

I really do not know how I could have gone through the previous evening and not realized the baby was not moving. As I recall the events from that day (and believe me, I can recall all the events from that entire week, right down to what I was wearing), I think that God must have had a reason for me not to have noticed until the next morning. Even at this moment, I choose to remember that His timing is perfect.

When I finally called the doctor to explain I had not felt the baby move, she advised me to do a kick count. A kick count is when you lie down and count how many kicks you feel in an hour. At this point in my pregnancy, she said I should feel a minimum of eight kicks in an hour. I was so frantic that my husband decided to come home early from work to sit with me while I counted kicks. It's a good thing he did. After lying there for an entire hour, I felt nothing, not one kick. I called the doctor back. She said to come in right away.

My heart was beating harder and faster than I had ever felt it beat before. My mind was racing uncontrollably, and I was short of breath as if I had run a mile. I was on the edge of a complete emotional breakdown.

When I arrived, a nurse led me into an exam room in the doctor's office. She then came in to listen to the baby's heartbeat. I am not sure how long it was that she listened for it, but it felt like an eternity. She could not find it, and my heart was pounding so hard that she was uncertain if it was the baby's heartbeat or mine she was hearing. She decided to use the ultrasound machine to enable her to see a picture of the baby.

The baby was lying still, and we had our worst fears confirmed. Our baby girl, our beautiful Courtney Elizabeth, whom we had been dreaming about for months, had no heartbeat.

After that, I know my doctor had a lot to say to me, but I remember none of it. I had the most wonderful Christian doctor, who said so many things to help me in the years to follow, but at that moment, I couldn't remember a single word she said. I was in shock and unsure that I had the strength to deal with losing my child. Soon afterward, she left the room to call the hospital and make arrangements for me to go in the next morning and have an induction.

After she left, something happened that I will never forget – something that redefined my marriage forever. My husband was sitting across the room from me. I sat up on the examining table, looked at him, and said, "I don't think I can do this." He stood up from his seat, walked across the room, gently took my face and lifted it up so that my eyes met his. He then responded to me and said, "We are going to do this

....

together." It was such a powerful moment. We were so young, and the world seemed to be collapsing all around us, but we were holding on to each other. Later, Paul told me that he made a decision right at that very moment that losing Courtney, as horrible as it was, was not going to destroy our marriage, and it most certainly was not going to define us. We were going to fight, and we were going to be okay.

God used my husband to help me grasp control and give me a sense of peace. There is nothing like the peace of God. I know, because I have experienced it. At the time of this tragedy, I was able to gain a very good perception of what my relationship with Jesus meant to me. At that moment, in that room, faced with that terrible news, I was reminded that I had made a commitment to follow Christ no matter what – and that here was where the rubber met the road. As I remembered that commitment, I was simultaneously reminded of His gifts. One of those gifts is the power of His peace. We only need to access it.

There is that word *only* again! It makes you think it should be easy. Peace is not normally something I am able to access easily. Yet in this instance, I was covered in it.

He gave me His peace just like He promised, and I trusted Him through the fire. Again, it was not easy. As time went on, I needed to be reminded daily to trust Him, but I made a choice to serve Him. It's all about choices. They make or break us – they decide our eternity.

Even though I left the doctor's office in a state of peace, I was still devastated. I liken the peace I had that evening to a pain medication; it took the edge off. I could still feel the pain, but I had a tool to manage it.

I called a close friend to give her the news, and I remember her saying, "I can't believe how calm you are." I said, "I could be angry and break every dish in the kitchen, but it wouldn't help." That night was a sleepless night. My pillow was tear-stained. I prayed and waited for my baby to "wake up" and miraculously move. She never did.

We had to be at the hospital the next morning at six. When we arrived and registered, we were assigned an elderly woman volunteer who showed us the way to our room. I then had my first experience with confessing the horror that my life had become over the previous twenty-four hours.

The sweet volunteer looked at me with kind eyes full of excitement and said, "Oh, you are going to have a baby today!" I will never forget the overwhelming sickness in the pit of my stomach when I had to tell her the baby was stillborn, and this was anything but a happy occasion. She did not know how to respond to me. In the days ahead, I learned that her response was not abnormal. There are no words for tragedy.

After admitting me to my room, the nurses settled me in and began the induction process. In a little over six hours, Courtney Elizabeth Kostick's tiny little body came into the world quiet and peaceful. I held her for four hours; she stayed warm in my arms. She looked like a little sleeping princess with rosy red lips and dark black hair. We did not have an autopsy done; I could not handle the thought of that. But her umbilical cord was much shorter than the average length, and the cord was twisted several times like a phone cord. It was presumed to be a cord accident, and that diagnosis was sufficient for us.

Shortly after giving Courtney to the nurses, my husband leaned his head on the side of my hospital bed and cried, "What did we do to deserve this?" He knew the answer to his own question as well as I did. The answer is nothing; we did nothing to deserve this. The facts are that I did not use drugs or alcohol during my pregnancy; I had excellent prenatal care and was careful about everything I did. We have a tendency to blame ourselves when bad things happen. We check and recheck everything that we could have possibly done. Then we start to believe lies from Satan, the father of lies, and that is where we can fall into trouble.

Let me tell you right now, if you are questioning yourself and taking blame after doing all the right things during your pregnancy: this is just a tactic from the enemy to keep you down. You must fight those feelings with prayer and scripture. Those are your weapons, and this is your war. You can win it. Jesus gave you the power when He died on the cross! Find a scripture to stand on, commit it to memory, and start battling. The scripture that helps me battle is Joshua 1:9: "Have I not commanded you? Be strong and of good courage; do not be afraid, or be dismayed, for the Lord your God will be with you wherever you go." Ephesians 6 says that the sword of the Spirit is the Word of God. Lose yourself in His Word and begin fighting. You must purpose to win!

7

Living the Nightmare

I refused to stay in the hospital that night because the sound of the crying from the babies being born into the world cut at my soul. My doctor reluctantly released me around 7:00 that evening. I went home, went to bed, and awoke the next morning to go look at cemetery plots. It was hard to believe this was really happening to me. After going to the cemetery, we stopped at the grocery store to purchase a few items. I was in pain since it was less than twenty four hours since I had a natural birth, and here I was on my feet feeling as if I had to keep busy.

While in the grocery store, I heard a baby cry; that was my first breakdown. I started to cry and took off as fast as I could out of the store. If you have had a baby, then you know the speed at which I was able to travel at that point… turtle speed. The cry sounding from that sweet baby was killing me, and it was a slow escape out the doors of the grocery store to my vehicle.

The next painstaking event was the following morning when my milk came in. In all the commotion of trying to plan a funeral and a reception, I was completely taken off guard. To be honest, I never even gave a thought to my milk coming in. It's like I forgot about that part because I had no baby to nurse. I woke up only to realize what was happening, and the heart-wrenching pain intensified. I did not believe it was possible to die of a broken heart until that moment. It was then that I thought I just might.

It seemed there were new hurdles to jump over every day. Going back to church was the next one I had to face. Going anywhere the first time after a tragedy is difficult. People aren't sure what to say to you or how to treat you. It is also very possible to have a public breakdown and expose yourself to the world. No matter how you look at it, it is a dubious situation. The first time I went to church after losing Courtney was nightmarish for me. It was stressful to get out of bed and have to put on what seemed like a pound of make-up in hopes of erasing the bags under my cried out, swollen eyes. Not to mention, the anticipation of how the congregation might react to seeing me was making me feel physically ill.

It was just as I thought it might be. Suddenly, everyone knew me "personally" and couldn't wait to hug me. I stood there with a smile on my face while thinking in my head, "Get away from me, you crazy people!" They were using phrases such as, "Here's my girl," and "You poor baby." I continued thinking, "Since when did I become your girl, and I am not a baby!" I knew they were trying to be kind and show support, but I just wanted to blend into the furniture.

I was so tired of people telling me that this was going to be part of my testimony someday, and that God was going to enable me to help others through experiencing this tragedy. Everyone who saw me said the same things. I was not ready to hear what they had to say, because I didn't want to accept that God actually had allowed this to happen. But... they were right.

God has used this horrific situation in my life for good. I found it too easy then to feel upset with people for offering what seemed to be generic advice. I wish that I could have at least tried to keep my heart open to what those individuals were saying. Some of those seemingly irrelevant pieces of advice that I lamented turned out to be the truth that kept me living from one daily miracle to the next.

It took some time to be understanding of people's attempts to try to make me feel better. One day, I grew so tired of the sad eyes and pitiful "I'm sorry's" that I took a different course of action. Weeks after that first day in church, my husband and I went to lunch with family when our waitress turned out to be an old acquaintance of my sister-in-law. The waitress knew that I was supposed to have just had a baby. She obviously didn't know the outcome. She gushed, "Aw, didn't you have a baby recently?" I calmly answered, "Yes, I did." She replied, "Oh, congratulations!" I said, "Thank you," with a giant smile on my face and my mind screaming to God, "Oh please, please, please, do not let her say anything else!" Dealing with this situation differently seemed pretty successful, which led to my thinking, Maybe there is something to be said for this "denial" stuff.

It was an escape for me to be able to "play it down" and pretend it didn't happen. But I must tell you that you cannot live in denial, though every once in a while you'll do what you think that you have to do. That was one of those times.

For a long time, every morning started the same. I woke up and for a fleeting half second thought that everything was okay, and then it all came flooding back to me. I remembered all of the brokenness. I remembered I was not pregnant. Worst of all, I remembered I was never going to bring my baby girl home. The pain was almost too much for me to bear. All I could think about was being pregnant again.

I tried to go on with normal daily activities, but my stress level was too high due to the trauma I'd faced. I could not focus on any one thing for very long. I started waking up in the night with crazy visions in my head. The scary part was that I wasn't sleeping and dreaming this. I was wide awake.

....

8

Hanging in the Balance

For God has not given us a spirit of fear,
but of power and of love and of a sound
mind. (2 Timothy 1:7)

My struggle with fear can be crippling. It would devour me if I allowed it. In the beginning days of my struggle after Courtney, my fear led to panic and anxiety. It started with simple thoughts. Slowly those thoughts began to penetrate my spirit and wedge themselves between God and me. Sometimes my anxiety led me to attacks where I could not catch my breath. During those attacks, I had trouble swallowing, and my heart would palpitate. I never knew when it would happen to me, so I started to fear that it would happen in front of people. For a time, I had to fight with myself to leave the house. I forced myself to continue living normally, but fear gripped me. I was in over my head.

I wanted my baby, and I would think about holding her. Sometimes I would think that I heard her crying, and then I would start to have visions of myself going to the cemetery in the middle of the night, and digging up her grave. I would see myself on my hands and knees with mud-covered fingernails and a tear-stained face as I desperately tried to claw my way to her lifeless body.

I was afraid I was literally going crazy, and for a short period of time, I just might have been. I almost hate writing this, because I have come so far from where I was then to where I am now. The girl on her hands and knees in the cemetery is practically unrecognizable. I can hardly believe it was me in that awful place of struggle, trying to identify what was real and what wasn't.

Because of this, I count it extremely important for you to know that, if you are in a dark place that can only be classified as nothing less than sheer torture, you need to believe that God wants you to have a sound mind. You need to, for lack of a better term, pull yourself up by your bootstraps and fight for your sanity. Depression can lead you into a pit that only Jesus can pull you out of. You might need to spend some time talking with someone. There is nothing wrong with seeking good, godly professional counseling. The important thing is that you recognize that you are fragile and that you reach out for help.

I wish I could say that every time I felt the anxiety and the "crazy" start to penetrate my thoughts I would quote scripture. I cannot. It took me a long time to break free of the chains of fear to where I could think straight enough to fight with the Word of God. If you are now where I was then, I want to remind you to quote 2 Timothy 1:7 every time you feel that awful anxiety start to take over. It may take time, but slowly it will take hold and you will begin to have a sense of peace.

I have said it before, and I will say it again: you need scriptures to stand on throughout this fight. The Bible is the living Word and a clear depiction of His love for you. Dig in, find a scripture to stand on, and fight the fear!

A huge part of helping me through my days was my son Pauly. He was such a cute little guy, and it would have been impossible for me to see those blue eyes and that sweet smile each day and not find joy. One definitive lesson I learned from my tragedy is the importance of joy. It took me time to reach that place in my life, and though I am not always successful, I really do try to find joy in every situation.

At night when my house is quiet and my husband's strong arms are keeping me warm, when everyone I love is safe, I am overjoyed and thankful. I am thankful for normal days. I do not feel the need to wish to be rich and famous or wish for anything at all out of the ordinary. The ordinary is just fine for me.

Part of the healing process is rediscovering joy. I had to learn to laugh again. The smiles that used to lead to hearty laughter were repressed in gloom, and I had to search deep within to find them. Laughter is key, and even while staring death squarely in the face, there is opportunity for laughter.

A few days after Courtney's funeral, I was still not able to sleep. I found myself pacing our tiny apartment throughout the night and then felt horrifically tired trying to take care of my son when morning approached. One afternoon my mother-in-law decided to drop over for a visit. Instead of showering me with cards and flowers like everyone else, she decided she would bring me the gift of sound sleep. From her purse, she pulled out a small bottle of over-the-counter sleep medication. As I crawled beneath the covers, she handed me a glass of water with a tiny pill and said, "This is going to help you sleep. But you know what? You should probably take two because they're small."

....

If you do not know where this is going, let me first say that just because a pill is small does not mean it is any less powerful than a horse pill! She drugged me! Unknowingly, of course. None of us was thinking very clearly those days. Needless to say, I slept for hours... and hours... and hours, until my stomach won the battle. I was starving! I fought myself awake enough to stumble to the kitchen, eat some cheese and crackers, and then hit the sack for the rest of the night. To tell you the truth, I haven't slept as well since.

The point is that, even though she accidentally drugged me, it was funny, and we still laugh about it today. It's okay to smile and even belly laugh in the midst of the nightmare you are living through wide awake. I honestly feel that God dropped that little bit of "funny" into our laps at the time, because we all sincerely needed it. I also needed the sleep.

Make me hear joy and gladness, that the
bones You have broken may rejoice.
(Psalm 51:8)

It's only fitting to save this verse for when I talk about joy. This entire psalm is incredible. It is a prayer of repentance from David after Bathsheba.

Many times when faced with devastation and adversity, we choose other things – addictions or anything else at all that will take us far from our trouble – instead of God. God wants us to turn to Him and allow Him to bring us joy on our journey.

David says, "Make me hear joy and gladness." Sometimes we have to cry out in all honesty and say to God, "Lord, make me do what is right, because I am filled with so much grief that I only want to do what is wrong. Lord, make me hear joy because I only hear sadness!" It's okay to be honest. He already knows the truth whether you admit it or not. If He has allowed us to be broken, it's for a reason. Do not try to figure it out. Rejoice in your brokenness. Take a moment, even if it's brief, to smile again.

I used several avenues to help in my healing process. I listened to a lot of worship music. I went to church every time the doors were open, and I made myself live even though at times, though I hate to admit it, I wanted to die.

When tragedies come in our path, it is absolutely incredible how we have been equipped by our God to deal with what we never thought we could. Have you ever watched the news or heard of something terrible that has happened to someone else and thought to yourself, "I could never live through that"? Well, I am a firm believer that God has enabled each one of us with strength to stand up to circumstances we never thought we could. If that horrible thing happens to you, then you can do all things through Christ who strengthens you. It is a biblical statement straight from Philippians 4:13. Although some might take the words *all things* in this scripture out of context, "all things according to His will" is what this means. Healing happens when we are living within His plan for our lives.

You can – and will – make it through this! The question is *how*. What will your choices be to lead you to a place of healing and contentment? I have already given you some examples of what helped me to heal, like worship music, going to church, and finding joy in what I already had. I also read my Bible a lot. However, I still made my share of mistakes and did not always handle my grief the way I should have.

Remember the prayer journal I told you about? Well, in one of my fits of rage, I tore it to shreds and threw it away. At times I would scream at my husband for no apparent reason. I also took things out on other family members. Some of my prayer conversations with my Lord even turned into one-sided screaming matches. I asked Him, "Why? How could You?" When I think of those hurtful words I uttered in my battered condition, I thank God for His mercy, understanding, and forgiveness.

In all this, deep in my heart, I remembered that too many people, when devastated by loss, will turn to all the wrong things before they turn to God, who loves them. I did not want to make that mistake. I needed Him. I also had to come to grips with the fact that, no matter how awful this calamity was, He allowed it to happen. I didn't understand why. Nonetheless it had happened, and I had no other choice but to trust Him.

How can we argue with God? He is all-knowing. He has every situation concerning our lives figured out, and we need to continue to trust in Him. He is not only the light at the end of the tunnel; He is the light in the tunnel, even if we cannot see it. It is all about faith, which is believing in things unseen.

I had to take my life back, and that started with gaining control of my anger. There were days when I was mad at the world. I hurt others in my fits of rage – rage born out of exasperation about my problems. I was tired of throwing tantrums and pity parties. It was time to grow up and get a grip.

9

Pressing in and Pressing on

Be angry, and do not sin. Meditate within
your heart on your bed, and be still. Offer
the sacrifices of righteousness, and put
your trust in the Lord. (Psalm 4:4-5)

I learned to communicate these two verses to myself whenever
anger and frustration stole the best of me. There were so many
days when I felt swallowed up by my circumstances. I am not
proud to admit that anger became a key emotion – second
only to the disappointment of being powerless to change the
outcome of my pregnancies. It was fundamental that I came to
an understanding that it was not okay for me to be angry at
God. I was like Jekyll and Hyde. One day I was okay with
accepting my circumstances, and the next I was in blame-God-
and-the-whole-rest-of-the-world mode.

I had to learn that I could not sin in my anger, and that
my pain could no longer excuse my anger. I had to put Psalm
4:4-5 into practice daily. I literally would go to my bed and
pray. I could not allow anger to rule my heart; I had to let God
rule my heart.

My prayer life was growing rapidly by leaps and

....

bounds through all of this. Even though it was difficult, I learned how beautiful prayer is – and how it connects you to the Father. Prayer is much like a battery charger. Your cell phone will not work if you do not charge the battery. If your battery were dead, you would have no means of communication to keep you updated. We cannot stay filled with the Holy Spirit without being in constant communication with the Father. Prayer recharges our souls.

The only way for me to find the strength that I needed to fight my battle every day was to dialogue openly with the Father. This translated into the privilege of falling more and more in love with Jesus. Even though I had questions, I had to continue my pursuit of Him to be able to live through the heartache.

So Jesus answered and said to them,
"Assuredly, I say to you, if you have faith
and do not doubt, you will not only do
what was done to the fig tree, but also if
you say to this mountain, be removed and
be cast into the sea, it will be done. And
whatever things you ask in prayer,
believing, it will be done."
(Matthew 21:21, 22)

God is so amazing! He has given us everything that we need to persevere. We only need to have faith and believe. Pay close attention to verse 22, where Jesus says, "Whatever things you ask in prayer." We need to make sure that our

....

prayer life is what it must be. Make an effort to know Him. Seek Him with your whole heart. To know Him is to love Him – more and more and more.

It is very hard to have faith in someone you do not know. When you grow closer to Him through your prayer life, your faith in Him will grow. A closer connection with Christ will provide the endurance you need to move the mountains.

In the midst of my heartbreak, I learned so much. Looking back, I wish I had responded the way God would have wanted me to. Recently, I reread the book of Job. His response in the face of adversity is jaw-dropping. As I was reading, a few verses jumped off the page to me in a way they never had before. In Job 1:13-19, Job learns of all he has lost. I find it interesting that the last piece of information he receives concerning his losses is the death of his children. Hearing this, Job descends into despair; yet in the middle of his heartbreak (verse 20), Job rises, tears his robe, shaves his head, and falls to the ground and worships. I cannot begin to express to you how that impresses me. Job responds exactly as he should.

I wish that upon finding out that Courtney was stillborn, in spite of my loss, my first response had been to bow on my knees and worship. Sadly, it wasn't. Yet what brings tears to my eyes in the story of Job is what happens next. Job says, "Naked I came from my mother's womb, and naked shall I return there. The Lord gave, and the Lord has taken away; blessed be the name of the Lord." And the most amazing response from Job is in verse 22: "In all this, Job did not sin nor charge God with wrong." Wow!

....

Unfortunately, I probably identified more with Job's wife throughout the beginning stages of dealing with loss. In Job 2:9, she advises Job just to curse God and die. When I think of Job's story, I think about what his wife must have been like and how much hurt she must have been enduring. Although we do not learn much about her, we know that she obviously felt the loss. After all, they were her children, too. Upon experiencing all that loss and watching her husband suffer with boils all over his body, she reacted wrongly. I wish that I didn't identify with her sin, but I do. I thank God for His mercy.

After losing Courtney, I faced emptiness much deeper than I had ever known. This pain travelled into my soul and left me feeling hollow inside. I felt unable to control the emotions that overtook me every day. The miscarriages had broken my heart, but this was even more difficult for me. I had felt every kick. I had seen the ultrasound pictures of her moving around inside of me. I had heard her heartbeat at every doctor's appointment. I had been connected to her not only physically, but emotionally. She was mine, and I was hers. I loved her as if I had known her for a lifetime.

One of the greatest difficulties of experiencing stillbirth is all the lost hopes and dreams of what could have been. To live forever wondering how your little one would have looked at a certain age or what talents he or she would have had can be torturous. Trust me when I tell you that, even though I have come to terms with my outcome, I still can drive myself crazy with wondering. I cannot wait to see that little girl's face in heaven, because I cannot stop thinking about what she looks like, and the joy the sound of her giggle must bring. Sometimes I find myself wondering whom she would have been friends with, and what her interaction with her brother would have been like. The "what ifs" of her life are still enough to make me crazy. I must remember that God is good all the time, and all the time God is good.

I play a little piano, and I sing, so a long time ago I wrote a song called "I Envision You." Some of the lyrics are, "I envision you laughing with me. I envision you talking to me. I envision you hugging and kissing, and then I start missing you. I envision you." You see, as the mother of a stillborn child, all I have is my own created visions of who she might have been.

In the midst of those lost dreams, I needed a lot more faith than I could have ever imagined. I had set out to have a second child, but so far had lost two babies to miscarriage and a beautiful daughter to stillbirth. When most mothers were picking out pink dresses, I was picking out a pink casket and headstone. My walk in the valley of the shadow of death had only just begun.

10

Infertility

Infertility is an arduous climb that makes everything ache.
Your body aches due to the process of treatment; your mind
becomes so focused on the task at hand (becoming pregnant)
that you cannot seem to remember the things that used to be
important. And worst of all, your heart aches. I mean it aches
incessantly, in a way that is completely indescribable to
anyone who has not experienced this type of pain. If you let it,
the agony of infertility and miscarriage will invade your being
like a disease.

Then the word of the Lord came to me,
saying: "Look, as the clay is in the potter's
hand, so are you in My hand, O house of
Israel!" (Jeremiah 18:5,6)

Among the ups and downs of grief, God was there
making me and molding me. It is the same for you. Right now,

....

at this very moment, He is making you and molding you into what He wants you to be. He says, "You are in My hand." What a powerful and beautiful statement.

I have a small figurine that I received as a gift. It is a little girl peacefully sleeping in a white hand. It was given to me to serve as a reminder that the babies I lost are in the hand of God. I use it as a reminder that I also am in His hands. I know my babies are safe and sound in His presence. I'm the one who feels lost at times.

As you are reading these words, remember that you, too, are in His hands. I have shared my struggle with anger; you might be facing the same struggle. When the clay is too hard, the potter has a very difficult time molding it. Do not allow your heart to grow hard just because the road is hard. Stay focused. I encourage you to find a visual aid that will jog your memory and remind you that you are in His hands.

Up to this point, I had a total of four pregnancies, which included one living child. I had not struggled to achieve those pregnancies. The longest time period it had taken to become pregnant was six months.

I had an urgent obsession to make right what went wrong. I had to fix this! The desire to control began taking hold, and my solution was to have another baby as fast as possible. Looking back, I cannot believe I thought I could replace Courtney. I was not processing my reality clearly. I was looking for a quick fix to ease my pain. Over time, I have learned I will never forget her, and the pain of losing her will never completely go away. God's grace helps me deal with my loss, and although time is helpful in the healing process, God has to be the one to fill the hollow soul and renew the spirit.

I immediately began trying to conceive again. The doctor advised me to wait three months or so, but I could think of nothing but being pregnant as soon as possible.

I went from starting my period every twenty-eight days to hardly ever having a period. I began to go months in between, and when I did have bleeding, it was usually just dark brown spotting. I was seeing my doctor often to try to figure it all out, and was usually found in her office dissolved in a puddle of tears before she could even say hello to me. I was a mess. Not only was I dealing with anxiety over having a stillborn daughter – I also was trying to come to terms with the two miscarriages previous to her. As if all that was not enough, I now added hormonal imbalances to my list of wounds. I was often heard asking aloud, "Dear God, what next?"

What actually did come next was the most exasperating situation I might have ever faced. Infertility was the next dart to wound my already broken heart.

For me, the one clear way to describe infertility is to picture being in a room with no doors, no windows, and no way out. The room is not dark; it is bright white, because then and only then are you aware that there is no means of escaping. Going over every square inch of the room with a fine toothed comb still reveals no way out. No matter what I did, I could not change it; I could not escape it. I had zero control over it. But it had one hundred percent control over me.

After trying to conceive for quite some time with no success, we opted to try Clomid. Clomid is a fertility drug that has high success rates and is inexpensive in comparison to most infertility medications. We had no success with this treatment. I then underwent surgery to remove cysts on my ovaries and check to see if my fallopian tubes were clear. After this, we still had no answers.

For those of you who have been trying to achieve pregnancy for any length of time, you know all the silly tricks: Change your husband from wearing briefs to boxers. Do not dare stand up right after intercourse, because you must put your legs in the air for a certain amount of time afterward (you have to make sure all those swimmers swim upstream). Oh my goodness, so stressful, so ridiculous! Forget enjoying each other. I was beginning to see myself as one big egg and my husband as one giant walking sperm. I was taking my temperature every morning and charting everything, and I mean everything! Some of you know what I am talking about. C'mon ladies, can I get an amen?

On the more serious side, these methods have proven to be successful for some people but never for me. I finally gave up and – go figure – almost two and a half long years since the death of our daughter Courtney, I finally became pregnant again.

11

Fifth Pregnancy

This time, I didn't have any signs to tell me I was pregnant. It was just a hunch. I still did not have regular periods, so it was impossible to tell whether I was late. I did take a home pregnancy test (probably my ten thousandth since starting this journey – I really should own stock in HPT), but the test was negative. I waited a few days and called the doctor. I went in for a blood test and found out the next day the results were positive, but the results were not altogether joyous. The problem was that my hormone levels of HCG were very low. It was a confirmed pregnancy, but we needed to wait and find out whether it was a very early pregnancy or a nonviable pregnancy. Two days later I started to bleed. Another baby lost and another broken dream.

This miscarriage happened on December 3, 1998, my son's sixth birthday. I was devastated by the fact that my son was already six years old and had no siblings. I put so much pressure on myself. I also kept thinking that my husband was such a wonderful father, and he could have had as many kids as he wanted if he had married someone else. This is an example of the lies of the devil that I wrote about earlier.

....

When we start buying into these lies, they change the way we feel about ourselves

The truth is that, in the end, it doesn't matter how we feel. We are not always going to feel good about ourselves. There will be days when we'll feel let down and beaten up by the world, but we will need to press on, fighting the good fight. We need to put on the full armor of God and walk in the knowledge that our lives are in the palm of His hand. If we serve Him, He will carry us through, regardless of how we feel. I will say it again: the key is faith, believing in things unseen.

After this miscarriage I again faced the ugly fear of infertility. It had taken well over two years to become pregnant this time, and I was terrified by the possibility that it could again take a significant amount of time to conceive. I really did not know how much more suffering I could handle. The peace I felt at the beginning seemed to be gone, and there was no end in sight.

12

The Battle Rages

We kept trying with no success. My doctor continually urged me to see an infertility specialist. I wanted to, but the cost prevented me. We decided to give it a try anyway to see what would happen and just hoped that we could swing it financially.

The first thing the specialists did was evaluate my medical history. They then began extensive testing to see if they could understand why I was having trouble with conception and why I kept miscarrying. Basically, the results showed no real reason why I should have miscarried. Irregular ovulation obviously had something to do with the infertility, but that was all that we knew. My thoughts were, "Great! Nothing serious that treatment can't fix!" Again, it is laughable that my mind was working this way. God opens and closes the womb. There is nothing wrong with seeking medical intervention, but ultimately God decides if the womb opens or stays closed. Bottom line. I was starting to trust in the doctors and in the treatment rather than in God. I cannot believe I hurt my Lord by putting faith in man rather than Him. If this is something you are struggling with, I urge you to please find a balance. I firmly believe that God has given medical experts knowledge to help us, but the decision is ultimately His. You cannot put your faith in anyone besides God.

> [Y]our faith should not be in the wisdom of
> men but in the power of God.
> (1 Corinthians 2:5)

It is important that we do not find ourselves so caught up in what the medical community tells us that we start putting faith in them rather than in God. Listen to what the doctors say, and do what you can to help yourself medically. But do not forget to give credit where credit is due. God alone opens and closes the womb.

> Heal me, O Lord, and I shall be healed;
> save me, and I shall be saved, for You are
> my praise. (Jeremiah 17:14)

I absolutely love this verse. Jeremiah is praying for deliverance and professing that if God chooses to intervene, the work is done. Jeremiah says, "Heal me, and I am healed. Save me, and I am saved." We need to cry out continually to Him, but our petitions should not become protests. We need to ask humbly; we don't need to defend ourselves or argue why He should answer according to our plan.

For years I was afraid the Lord was on His throne thinking, "I know, Jennifer, you have asked me for this same thing a countless number of times. Move on to something else, girlfriend. I'm tired of hearing it!" Wrong! Our prayers do not fall on deaf ears. He hears our desires and understands our pain. Remain humble and have the insight to recognize that, yes, God hears, and when He decides the time is right, then and only then will it be done. Until that day, He is making the path, and we must make the decision to follow it.

Last, I want to address the end part of the verse: "You are my praise." This is so beautiful to me, simply because praise is beautiful. Praising Him causes the weak to become strong; it causes the hard-hearted to become soft and makes the harsh winds of life turn into gentle breezes. Praise is our comfort, and He is our praise. I am convinced that our praise of Him is a primary step in moving mountains.

It can be hard to comprehend God, because as humans we need something tangible. We need to be able to reach out and touch Him, and when we feel God is untouchable, and that we cannot connect with Him because we cannot see Him, we hurt Him and we hurt ourselves. Here's the reason: He is the healer, the mountain mover, giver of life, and the One and only One who has any power to change anything.

The fertility doctors decided to try shots of medication to help me ovulate followed by insemination. This process is

....

referred to as IUI, which stands for intrauterine insemination. Basically, you take the same type of medications given for someone going through in vitro fertilization but in lesser doses. These particular injections of medication cause the body to produce several eggs at once, which increases your chance of achieving pregnancy. Ultrasounds are done regularly, and when ovulation is detected, doctors take the sperm which has been collected and washed in a special solution, puts it into a catheter, and threads it into the uterus, hoping the sperm will meet the egg and conception will take place.

This is an expensive process, mostly because of the medications. Our insurance did not cover any infertility treatment, and at the time, the medication alone for one week was around seven hundred dollars. This brought a whole new level of stress into the situation. We tried this process twice and both times failed. We could not afford to continue so we stopped, and I cried. Hard. I did not know it was possible for one person to shed so many tears.

13

Sixth Pregnancy

After giving up hope of conception per the infertility doctors, I enrolled in a kickboxing class at my church. I was trying to make some healthy changes in my life. Within just a couple weeks of taking the classes, I was feeling very nauseated. I remember going into the bathroom to throw up after class thinking I had simply worked out too hard. Before long, I constantly felt nauseated. When I called Paul at work crying that there was something physically wrong with me, he was convinced I was pregnant and insisted I take a pregnancy test. I felt like I was dying. Yes, you probably guessed it – the feeling of morning sickness.

I fought taking a pregnancy test, because I felt like I could not handle one more disappointment. It pained me to think of another negative result. However, I finally heeded my husband's advice and bought the test. I was so tired of being a slave to those pink test lines. Those stupid, God-forsaken, ridiculously overpriced little pink lines that I somehow thought held the fate of my whole existence. How can anything that you pee on actually hold that much value? Anyway, you can imagine the shock I had when the result was positive! I danced around my house for joy holding that little peed-on stick because at that moment those two little pink lines were the most beautiful sight I had seen in quite some time. After the dancing ceased, I decided to call my infertility doctors because they had been involved with my case most recently. The doctor agreed to see me, and the next day I went in for an ultrasound. I was six weeks and four days pregnant, and everything looked great.

Within a week after the ultrasound I started some light spotting. This was a very different experience for me, because with all three of my previous miscarriages, I was never sick. I was hoping and praying it would pass. I kept telling myself that a lot of women have spotting during their pregnancies and things turn out fine. After all, I saw the ultrasound myself; I was told the pregnancy was healthy. In fact, I was told the baby was in a perfect position in the uterus; not to mention, the morning sickness was stronger than ever.

It was a Saturday night. In the middle of the night I awoke from a sound sleep to use the bathroom when I noticed a lot of blood in the toilet. I yelled for my husband, told him what was happening, and asked him for a drink of water. Slowly, I stood to my feet and stepped into the hallway. Suddenly, I felt very weak, and the next thing I remember is waking up to my panic-stricken husband yelling my name. He called an ambulance, and I was taken to the hospital. At that point there was nothing to be done. The heavier bleeding turned back to a light spotting. The hospital sent me home with instructions to follow up with my doctor.

Because the infertility specialist was following my case, I was able to schedule an appointment the next day, which was Sunday. (Infertility doctors are there every day of the week.) The doctor did an ultrasound and the baby looked great. I was put on bed rest in hopes that the spotting would stop. I went home and straight to bed.

Later the same evening I needed to use the bathroom. When I first stood up, I felt a swishing sensation in my vaginal area. Before I could even think about it to pinpoint what it might be, the hemorrhaging started. There was blood everywhere. Paul did not want to take any chances waiting for an ambulance, so he picked me up, put me in the car, and rushed me to the hospital himself.

By the time we arrived at the hospital, I was starting to feel as if I was fading in and out. The nurse took us right back to triage. I was losing a lot of blood, and the nurse was asking a lot of questions. I had a blanket over my lap while she was trying to evaluate if the situation was as grave as I said it was. She realized it was when I passed out. I woke up vomiting. Next thing I knew, several doctors and nurses were picking me up, putting me on a bed, and strapping an oxygen mask over my face. It was one of the most frightening experiences of my life, and one I will never forget.

It took some time before I was stable. The hospital staff was working on preparing an operating room for a D&C. After spending the night in the hospital, I was released home the following morning on two weeks of bed rest. I was very anemic and needed to rest in order to bring my blood cell count back up to where it needed to be. I did not want a blood transfusion, so it was extremely important that I listened to everything they told me to do in order to avoid it, and I did.

All health issues aside, there was the realization that another baby had been ripped from my womb. I felt exhausted, not just because of the physical ramifications from the recent miscarriage, but from everything that we had endured over the last eight and a half years, since that first miscarriage. It was the year 2001, over five years since we had lost Courtney. My son Paul was nine years old, and I was nearing my twenty-ninth birthday.

14

Fighting to Stand Upright

How in the world was it possible for a couple to survive what we suffered and keep faith? How was it possible for me to be able to make a decision that, no matter what, I was going to fight? It is only through God! I wish I could say I gave Him my burden and never took it back, but the truth is, as it is for most Christians, that it was a daily process. I made a new decision every day to give my burdens to Jesus and allow Him to work in my heart. Every day I fought depression, weakness, and self-pity. I constantly fought thoughts that told me I would never again experience a healthy pregnancy and a healthy child. I even fought intense horrible thoughts that something would happen to the healthy child I did have.

Do you recall, from the introduction, the automobile accident that my husband was in with his brothers? Well, my son Pauly was in that car. He was the other passenger, and though he only sustained minimal injuries, I became caught in a new web of fear so intense that I was losing all semblance of who I once was.

I had so much fear at times that I would lie awake at night riddled with anxiety, but I kept giving Him the burden. I kept going through the process. It's all part of the healing. It's okay to break down; it wouldn't be normal not to have moments of complete mental exhaustion. What is not okay is to give yourself over to the feelings that this awful thing that is happening to you is your fault and that you must have done something to deserve this kind of pain. Be very careful to separate yourself from thoughts that wrongly accuse you and make you the problem.

He heals the brokenhearted and binds up
their wounds. (Psalm 147:3)

When we have a cut or a scrape, we are careful to keep it clean in order to lessen our chances of infection. But what happens when we have a broken heart? How do we keep out infection? If we are not careful to keep our hearts clean when we are hurt, we have a tendency to allow bitterness to come in and infect our very souls.

So many of us could easily be classified as "walking wounded." We have been beaten up by our circumstances and, in the process, created an opening for bitterness to seep in and infect us. Keeping our hearts pure before God allows Him to be able to work in us and bind up our wounds. Yes, it is true He heals the brokenhearted, but those of us suffering from broken heartedness need to allow Him to minister His love to us, so that we might be healed.

Take comfort that He heals the brokenhearted, but take heed that we must keep our hearts right in order for Him to be able to bind up our wounds! Sometimes I would walk up

....

to the altar during ministry time at church, lift my hands, and sing Him praises. Honestly, most of the time I was making myself do it. It was a process for me out of obedience to Him. I had to go through the motions of giving myself completely over to Him before I could actually do it. Sometimes we just need to go through the steps.

I have a method to remind myself of His overwhelming faithfulness. It helps me overcome insecurities, of which I have plenty. I tape scriptures and quotes in places where I can see them. When I catch a glimpse of those reminders taped up around my home, it helps me exercise faith. It takes work to put faith into practice.

God has a perfect plan and will for your life; you are precious to Him. Give Him your burden every day, and one morning soon you will wake up with a renewed sense of hope and peace. A new day is coming – a day when you will realize that yesterday you gave Him the same old burden, and that for the first time, you have not taken it back!

> They have bowed down and fallen; but we
> have risen and stand upright. (Psalm 20:8)

When I first read this scripture by itself, I focused on the physical act of standing upright and what that means – perpendicular, vertical. I also envisioned enemies such as heartache and rejection dropping one by one, but none of that really sat well with me. Then I started looking up synonyms for the word upright, which are true, honorable, and virtuous, just to name a few.

....

Standing upright is so much more than just position; there is an important correlation between the two meanings. I want to stand upright in the sight of the Lord. I want to be true, I want to be honorable, and I want to be virtuous. I want to spend my life fusing myself more and more into who Christ is, and I want to rid myself of my selfishness.

It is only when we stand upright in the spiritual realm that we have hope of standing upright in the physical. Focusing on God and taking the focus off our problem helps us to stand upright.

15

Seventh Pregnancy

More than a month after the last miscarriage, I was going on with my regular day-to-day activities. I was trying to concentrate on recovering physically, but I could not seem to shake the tiredness. It was now the beginning of December 2001. I hadn't had a period since the miscarriage, which was not completely abnormal for my body, but the feeling I had was all too familiar. This time, I headed straight to the pharmacy for another home pregnancy test.

I told myself I was just checking so I could rule it out, not because I thought I really was pregnant. Surely, after all the time it took me to become pregnant, I could not possibly be pregnant again so soon. My body just didn't work like that anymore. I was wrong.

I was pregnant again. I have no idea how it happened so quickly. For years my body revolted against me by not allowing me to ovulate properly, and now twice in a row everything worked. To communicate with you that roller coaster ride of emotions is impossible. I had absolutely no clue how to feel about this pregnancy. I was afraid of becoming too attached, but how could I not be? After hemorrhaging the last time, I was now concerned for my life. My husband was overwhelmed with worry, my highly emotional Italian mother was terrified, and I was convinced that if this pregnancy didn't kill me, she just might! Shock and awe were pretty much the consensus, but as I have said before, it really doesn't matter how you feel. You trust God; there is no other way!

I once again called the infertility doctors. I had an early ultrasound which showed a healthy little heartbeat. I was scared, yet was choosing to believe every moment that my cries had been heard and life would finally go our way.

Did you notice I used the word *choosing*? We must choose to believe, because otherwise we will live in constant fear and doubt. This is one way to battle these feelings. Also, I say "our," because as women when we are experiencing all these terrible circumstances, we can forget that our husbands feel just as terrible. It might be our bodies dealing with the physical pain, but they are watching and are helpless to do anything but pray. Please do not forget that our husbands walk the same journey.

It is too easy to become selfish and wrapped up in our own world of trouble. We can sometimes feel that we are the only ones hurting. But He is also hurting, and we need to remember that. My husband loves making me happy. Ephesians 5:25 says, "Husbands, love your wives, just as Christ loved the church and gave himself up for her." My husband takes this scripture very seriously, and I know he loves me very much. He is a great support, and I am ashamed to say that when I was hurting I made it all about me way too often, even though he was hurting just as much. At times, I have thought he may have been bruised more deeply than I, because he had to watch someone he loved very much fall apart physically and self-destruct emotionally.

....

He deserves a lot of credit for loving me through that difficult time. Try not to forget that your husband could be hurting more than you can imagine. Men typically do not exude the same type of behavior women do, so it may be more difficult to recognize, but do not cast him off. He needs love and encouragement as well. Men sometimes have a strong tendency to want to fix things, especially when the circumstances affect people they love. When he cannot repair the situation, he feels frustrated and powerless, just as bad as or worse than we do when experiencing the same situation.

I was about seven weeks along when, once again, the spotting started. I had also started throwing up, and the more I threw up, the more I bled. Because of what I had experienced with the previous miscarriage, being sick this time was not a comfort. I had no idea what would happen and no innocence left to shield me from reasoning out the situation. I felt terrible. I looked terrible. I was very anemic, because my body hadn't recovered fully from the blood loss from the previous miscarriage, and yet again, I found myself begging God to give me a miracle.

My regular ultrasounds all showed that, regardless of the bleeding, the baby was developing normally. At nine and a half weeks, the bleeding began to increase, so I had to have another ultrasound to check on the baby. During the process, I could sense there was something different about the doctor's temperament, so I asked her, "Do you see a heartbeat?" She said, "Yes, I do," and proceeded to tell me that the baby was funneling.

This was a new one for me. I had no idea what she meant. What was funneling? Basically, the baby had moved down and my cervix was opening up. Around twenty minutes later, I went to the bathroom and the whole sac, baby and all, slipped right into the toilet.

The only way for me to describe the feeling of my baby slipping from my body into a toilet is with the word *violated*. I felt violated. There was no one personally responsible for this, and yet I felt as if someone ripped him out of me. The reason I say him is because we had genetic testing done on the fetus to try to figure why I miscarried. We never found out why, but we did learn that it was a little boy. I wished I didn't know. It only made it hurt worse. Following the miscarriage, the bleeding didn't stop as quickly as the doctors would have liked, so they sent me for a D&C.

I was done. I needed a break. It was too much for me to handle, and my husband said he could not and would not watch me suffer the physical or emotional pain any longer. His words were, "Enough is enough; we're done."

After this, we were careful to use methods of birth control for about six months. I then decided that I would really like to at least entertain the thought of trying again, but convincing my husband was another story. I know it must sound crazy that, after all we had been through, I would even begin to surrender to the thought of another pregnancy, especially after losing so much blood and risking my health the way I had. I can only say that I was obsessed. I wanted a baby so badly that it did not matter to me what I had to do. No one could reason with me, because I was desperate. Desperate people do desperate things.

16

Giving of Yourself to Bring Him Glory

My periods were still irregular, so we knew the chances of conception again on our own were probably slim. The only way to convince Paul to go along with my insanity was promising "no more looking at calendars and trying to track dates, no more taking my temperature, and no more ovulation kits." If it happened again on its own, then we would be thankful while hoping and praying for a miracle.

During this time we decided to move back to Pennsylvania to be near my family. When we relocated we were busy building a home, involving ourselves in a new church, and taking on new ministry opportunities. I rarely had time to dwell on the fact I was not becoming pregnant. It would still cross my mind every so often, and when I thought about it hard enough I could hear the familiar, desperate cry from my heart to have a baby. I still had the desire, so my new prayer was, "God, please take the desire to have another baby away from me."

May He grant you according to your
heart's desire, and fulfill all your purpose.
(Psalm20:4)

I believe very strongly that He will grant the desires of
our hearts if the desires we seek are godly. I have a friend who
lost a baby boy to stillbirth. She decided to adopt two beautiful
daughters the Lord had handpicked just for her. Her desire
was not fulfilled the way she had expected at the beginning of
her quest for a child, but they were granted just the same. And
because the desire was God-centered, these girls are far above
and beyond the most precious gifts that she could have ever
dreamed.

When you truly submit your heart and life to Christ,
you begin to desire the things of Him. You open up your soul
and allow it to be transformed by the power of His will. At
that time, all things that He desires you desire as well. This is
because He places the desires in your heart at the time of
surrender.

Our human spirit may have a hard time deciphering
these desires, which is why sometimes we end up with
something different from what we expected, but we never end
up disappointed. His will is always better than our own. Have
peace, knowing that He will grant your desires and fulfill your
purpose – when your desires are His.

He did not take away my desire to have another child,
but He did fill my life with wonderful new projects, new
people, and new purpose. I learned that we must have a
purpose. God gave each one of us talents and gifts that are
meant to glorify Him.

....

More than ever, the scriptures that God had spoken to me through the years of devastation were making sense.

And you shall remember that the Lord
your God led you all the way these forty
years in the wilderness, to humble you and
test you, to know what was in your heart,
whether you would keep His
commandments or not. So He humbled
you, allowed you to hunger, and fed you
with manna which you did not know nor
did your fathers know, that He might
make you know that man shall not live by
bread alone; but man lives by every word
that proceeds from the mouth of the Lord.
Your garments did not wear out on you,
nor did your foot swell these forty years.
You should know in your heart that as a
man chastens his son, so the Lord your
God chastens you. Therefore you shall
keep the commandments of the Lord your
God, to walk in His ways and to fear Him.
For the Lord your God is bringing you into
a good land, a land of brooks of water, of
fountains and springs, that flow out of
valleys and hills; a land of olive oil and
honey; a land in which you will eat bread
without scarcity, out of whose hills you can
dig copper, When you have eaten and are

....

full, then you shall bless the Lord your
God for the good land which He has given
you. (Deuteronomy 8:2-10)

When I was in the desert, the Lord wanted me to yield
fruit. He did not want me to wander aimlessly while waiting
for Him to provide my miracle.

In my Bible, I have a note in the margin next to these
scriptures. It is dated 2-1-98 and says: "The Lord has tested me
and brought me through. All the time He was preparing me
for my gift." Even though he had not provided the end result I
wanted, He still brought me to a place of realizing that He had
given me specific gifts that were to be used to give Him glory.

You may feel as if you are in a desolate place, lifeless
and gloomy. It does not have to be this way. Right now in
your state, you can yield fruit. You can accomplish this by
using your gifts to praise Him along the way. Show others
your unwavering faith.

In this passage from Deuteronomy, the Lord showed
me that He was going to give me strength to handle the
difficult road, just as He showed the children of Israel that He
was going to bring them out of the wilderness and into a good
land.

He was teaching them to praise Him along the way.
We need to give back to Him. We don't praise Him only
because of the blessings He can bestow, but simply because He
is God. In the midst of our trials, He continually reveals
Himself to us. We must be obedient! We must respond to Him!
Whatever gift you have came from Him. Use it for Him! Let it
become your outlet. Have faith that your God-given ability,
whatever it might be, will lead you closer to Him. Step out in
faith, and be productive. Do not be satisfied to attach yourself

to grief. Allow Him to prepare you for your gift and your future in Him.

Using your talents and gifts to touch the lives of others is a beautiful part of the healing process. We all have a calling; we all have a gift. Many times, if not at all times, our gifts directly relate to our story. Use them to glorify God and you will find purpose. As you find purpose, healing will begin.

I realized that by spending all my time concentrating on trying to have a baby again, I was not fully appreciating the child I already had. I love my son! Like any good mother, I would die for him, but for some reason I was so caught up in my obsession. It was like spending years on a merry go round just watching all the people go by. I did not want to feel as though I watched my son and my husband from the sidelines. I did not just want to go through the motions of everyday life; I wanted to actually enjoy it. It was time to pray for God's will and not my own. It was also time to find healing in my story.

> And Peter said to him, "Aeneas, Jesus Christ heals you. Arise and make your bed." Then he arose immediately. So all who dwelt at Lydda and Sharon saw him and turned to the Lord. (Acts 9:34, 35)

I don't know about you, but I want to jump out of my chair and worship after reading this! Not so much because of the healing, but about the reference that all who saw Aeneas turned to the Lord.

....

This bedridden man was suddenly and amazingly healed. However, this story tells me about more than physical healing. Remember when I said that we all have a story? I may not have been bedridden, but I was unable to produce another child, paralyzed and powerless to change my situation. Much like this bedridden man Aeneas, I was waiting for healing and deliverance, but I discovered that I did not need to have the result that Aeneas had to tell my story and make a difference in someone else's life. Putting the pieces of your life together after being broken can be more inspiring than the big end miracle you are praying for. It's the small miracles along the way that show others they can maneuver their way through the darkness.

Telling someone your story allows Jesus to be glorified! Find the good inside the bad and run with it; do not allow it to be for nothing. You do not need to have the end you are hoping for to impact people for Christ. He has already done a work in you. My doctor in California told me that she would encourage her other patients with my story. She would tell them of the faith I had to have another baby. At the time, I did not even realize I had much faith at all, or that my story was worth sharing. She helped me open my eyes and realize that I could have a testimony even though it seemed sorrowful. You never can be sure of the impact you will have on someone else. Share your story; maybe you will be someone's Aeneas! They will see you and turn to the Lord.

I had to make a point of saying constantly, "Lord, Your will be done, not my own." The more I said it, the more I believed it and actually wanted it. Through this, I was finally able to surrender control to Him and keep from focusing so much on the outcome of my story. I was learning to focus on all that God did in my life during those difficult days. Trust

....

me when I say that when it comes down to it, you always want it God's way, never your own. If it is your will and not His, you will be disappointed every time.

Though I was happy, content with my son and husband and with the fact that God had a plan separate from mine, my heart still panged as people around me had babies. This can be the hardest hurdle to jump. Watching pregnant women carry to term and watching pregnant women suffer a loss can lead to several scary emotions.

Rejoice with those who rejoice, and weep with those who weep. (Romans 12:15)

Let's first deal with this issue: Rejoice with those who rejoice. When you want a baby more than anything else in the world and see women having them all around you, you can begin to feel that those women are somehow undeserving. This is shaky ground. You cannot associate your situation with others'. The day of my daughter Courtney's funeral, my pastor at the time said something very wise to me, and it has stuck with me always. He said, "There is an evil woman out there somewhere today having a healthy baby. Direct your anger at the right source, not at God." It is Satan who came to steal, kill, and destroy. Be careful not to become full of anger toward God or others, just because they can have a baby and you cannot.

During the births of all five of my sister-in-law's children, I was a support person in the delivery room. During her first three deliveries, I was trying desperately to become pregnant. Throughout her first pregnancy, I was on fertility medications. It was extremely difficult for me to commit to be there for her, but I was being obedient to what I know God wanted to use me for. Through it, He brought healing.

It will never be easy to go to someone else's baby shower when you feel empty due to a loss or infertility. I know it isn't because I did it. It is horrible to put a smile on the outside and pretend everything is fine while screaming and crying on the inside. But don't ignore the invitations; go to the showers and hospital visits. Be whatever support that is required of you at the time. Be obedient and be blessed. Have faith and overcome.

The second – and possibly the most important – part of this scripture, is "weep with those who weep." Do not allow yourself to be at peace with the philosophy that "misery loves company." Pray for a healthy mom and baby concerning another's pregnancy. When you feel alone in a situation, evil thoughts can invade your mind.

For a while after losing Courtney, I would look at pregnant women and think about how they might deal with the loss if it were to happen to them. I hated feeling as if I was the only one who had ever lost a baby. It wasn't fair! You know what? Life isn't fair. I had to repent. Selfishness can lead to an indulgence of the flesh. Impede selfishness at all costs, and, if – God forbid – someone else sustains a loss while you are suffering, then weep with them, for them. Do not welcome embittered company.

In my heart, I genuinely wanted to be happy for those around me who were blessed with a new baby, and I wanted more than anything to move on with my life. But no matter how much I wanted that, I could not move on. For some reason the desire never went away. I worked hard to stay busy with other tasks that I felt God wanted me to do in an attempt not to obsess again. And then, just as I thought I was finally making progress, my grandmother was diagnosed with terminal cancer.

17

Try, Try Again

I was blessed with a wonderful grandmother. She passed
away in the year 2007 from breast cancer, and because we
were very close, it hurt me deeply when she passed away.
Before she died, though, she shared with me everything that
she felt she needed to say. Those final conversations with her
were gifts from the Heavenly Father. I will never forget the
beautiful things she said to me.

One of the topics was, of course, having another baby.
She told me I needed to let go of my fear. She said I was a
wonderful mother, and that it would be a shame for me not to
try at least one more time to have another child. After she
passed away, I could not stop her words from playing over
and over again in my head. Day and night I wondered what I
should do, and I called my new obstetrician/gynecologist,
who recommended I see a specialist. At first, this roused new
fears for me to fight.

When I have difficulty fighting fear, it always helps to
remember that I am not alone and that there is nothing new
under the sun. My favorite New Testament character is the
apostle Paul (formerly Saul). I marvel at the course his life

took. In the midst of the changes in Paul's life, God used a godly man named Ananias, a faithful servant at Damascus, in a mighty way.

Because of his apprehension about God's commandments, I feel a sort of kinship to Ananias. More importantly, because of his obedience through that apprehension, his story shows me that even the strongest Christians, handpicked by God Himself to assist in miracles, fought fear – just like me.

> Then Ananias answered, "Lord, I have heard from many about this man, how much harm he has done to Your saints in Jerusalem. And here he has authority from the chief priests to bind all who call on Your name." (Acts 9:13,14)

The rest of the chapter explains that even though Ananias was more than willing to do what the Lord asked of him, he still had fear about doing it. He said to the Lord, "[Saul] has authority from the chief priests to bind all who call on Your name." Still, the Lord told him to go, and out of obedience, regardless of his own apprehension, he went. He met Saul and prayed for him to receive his sight and be filled with the Holy Spirit.

I remember when I felt the timing was right to try to have another baby. I could almost feel a physical nudging deep within my soul. God told me two things: number one, I would need to tell my husband, but He would do the convincing; number two: I would need extreme medical intervention to help me.

Entangled in this new phase, I felt mixed emotions. On one hand, if God was leading me in this direction, then of course, it would work out for our good. On the other hand, my fear of disappointment was awakening old senses that told me to back off and keep going the way I was, continuing to pretend I did not need any more children. In other words, I would be living the same old lie.

Like Ananias, you may feel apprehensive. God might be speaking something to you, and you might find that you are afraid to pursue it. If you feel certain that God is leading you in a specific direction, whether it be adoption or infertility treatment, do not be afraid. If He leads, then you must follow. In the above passage, when the Lord first calls Ananias's name in a vision he responds, "Here I am, Lord" (verse 10). Isn't that what we all should be saying? Here I am, Lord.

As you can imagine, my husband was not at all happy about my wanting to try again to conceive. He worried about my health, both physically and emotionally, and he had every reason to. He was scared to death that another pregnancy "gone wrong" could cause me to hemorrhage and succeed in killing me. He also feared that making a decision to pursue infertility treatment again would open up the floodgates for more heartache. I asked him if he would at least pray about it. He said, "I don't want to." I asked, "Why? Are you afraid God will tell you, 'yes'?" He looked at me and smiled. Three days later he came to me and said, "You can make the call to the

....

doctor; God gave me peace." I made the call that same day,
and there began a chapter of our story that would change our
lives forever.

18

Sheer Desperation

The first appointment at the specialist went smoothly. The doctor looked over my medical records, which was no easy task considering my history, and suggested a round of tests required before we could decide on a course of treatment. Over the next couple months we completed all the required tests, and the results were more of the same. Everything looked great. The doctors were unable, based on my records and results from the new tests, to find any reason why I could not achieve pregnancy or stay pregnant. Generally, the more miscarriages you have, the more you can have, but there was no evidence to say I could not carry a baby to term.

We agreed with the physician's advice that in vitro fertilization seemed like the best course of action, due to the number of years we had been trying and my age. I was now thirty-four. It was the year 2007, and our son was already fourteen years old. This was going to be it for us. The very last try.

God seemed to be opening all the doors. The grandest entryway was our financial situation. The company where Paul worked had a wonderful medical insurance plan that covered up to twenty thousand dollars of infertility treatment, including medication. With the financial burden out of the way, we began our first IVF cycle.

If you are considering IVF, then you are probably desperate. To be straight forward, there's no way to explain a couple's reasons for going through IVF except sheer desperation. Like I shared before, desperate people do desperate things.

Paul and I had moral concerns about the fate of leftover embryos that need to be frozen. We also had to decide what we thought about the possibility of transferring embryos that might not implant. To us it would still be a sorrowful loss of life. We believe that life begins at conception, even if that conception takes place in a laboratory dish.

Some trust in chariots, and some in horses; but we will remember the name of the Lord our God. (Psalm 20:7)

I first memorized this scripture while volunteering at a children's vacation Bible school for the church we attended. This was the theme scripture, and someone wrote a catchy little jingle for it. While I wrestled with my emotions, unsure whether I would ever have peace in my heart again, God spoke to me through this scripture. I could not push the melody of the jingle out of my head. The song played repeatedly in my mind.

It struck me that regardless of the situation, there is no one I can trust in fully, except for the Lord my God. I must have read that verse a thousand other times, but it was only when I saw it through a child's perspective that the verse actually spoke to me. Too many times we adults make things overly complex. We need to have a childlike faith.

Through all our questioning, soul searching, and praying, feeling comfortable with undergoing this procedure came down to one thing: we felt the peace of God in the entire decision. It was vital to feel His peace in order to move forward, because despite whether IVF results in a healthy pregnancy, it will change your life.

The process of IVF has the potential to let you sink into despair. Things will not always go your way. There are gray areas, and at times your body fails you. I cannot begin to imagine living out the process of IVF without a relationship with the Lord. I know people do it every day, but it is unfathomable for me.

I didn't know before how overwhelming the process of IVF can be. I wish that I had known someone who had undergone IVF, and that I had done more research before beginning. For some reason, I had a daydreamer's attitude about the process. Because I had already been pregnant, I somehow believed this procedure would be easy for me. I figured that if my ovaries could be stimulated by the proper medications, then I would be "home free." At the beginning, I looked at all the positive aspects and none of the negative ones. It is a balancing act worthy of Olympic competition to have the faith to believe for the positives and still remain realistic and provide yourself the mat to fall on so you don't hit the concrete.

Along with the complicated emotions and moral dilemmas, IVF comes with lots of legal issues to consider. You must sign documents that dictate what happens to the embryos if frozen, where they will remain frozen, and who will inherit them if you and your husband die or divorce. This is nothing to take lightly. IVF is not a decision that is made on a whim.

I received several injections in my midsection every day. These medications should stimulate ovulation, but cause you to experience extreme emotional highs and lows. My husband deserves a lot of credit for handling my mood swings with ease. IVF also requires regular ultrasounds and blood work so that the doctors can detect the hormone levels and see how many follicles are developing on the ovaries. I felt like a pincushion.

The only thing that carried me through was my new prayer: "Lord, please make a way where there is no way." It became a lifeline for me, just like I had known before, when I had prayed that God's will be done, not my own. However, those are words that are never easy to confess. Let's face it; to accept His will sometimes means death to our own dreams. In the end it's always better, but the process of understanding why is painful.

19

Keep On, Keeping On

My first cycle of IVF did not show promising blood work or ultrasounds. My hormone levels were low, and I had very few follicles on my ovaries. The doctor was concerned that, because of my low hormone levels, the few follicles that were growing might not even contain eggs. My doctor suggested that we switch to an IUI cycle, the same infertility treatments I had undergone while living in California. I was devastated. Reluctantly, we converted the IVF cycle to an IUI cycle.

Two weeks later, I found out I was not pregnant. This time, I felt strong and more prepared to accept God's will for me. I can't say I liked it, but I was ready to accept it. This new turn of events broke my heart, but I was not ready to quit. For some reason, I felt God urging me to keep going on and keep trusting Him. This feeling was different from the obsession I had previously felt, and His peace was still showing strong in my soul.

Not that I speak in regard to need, for I have learned in whatever state I am in, to be content. (Philippians 4:11)

This, friends, is a tough one! Finding contentment on the slippery slope of misery and heartbreak . . . ugh, sigh! It took me years to feel as if I was nearing a glimpse at contentment with my life as it was. When I finally came to terms with the fact that I may never have more children, and that my son just might end up an only child after all, God strengthened my desire and opened the doors for IVF. If I had to go back and endure it again, I would hope to have wisdom enough to know that God placed me there for His purpose, even if I did not recognize what that purpose was. Hindsight is always 20/20. It saddens me to know that I spent so much time walking against the current.

I was hoping against hope that this treatment would succeed. IVF is the most advanced infertility treatment, so how could it not work? Right? Wrong! Here, I came to a new crossroads. I had learned to trust Him through loss, and now I had to trust Him through the process of IVF. I thought I had already come to that conclusion, but as the procedure became even more complicated, I had to consider things in a new light. In the midst of the questions, the Lord showed me that I needed to press on and pray for Him to make a way where there was no way. To be entirely honest, the fight was difficult some days, if not most, because I could feel myself slowly sinking into that old, familiar depression.

....

On top of all this, I finally had a diagnosis for my infertility problems. My diagnosis was diminished ovarian function. This meant that my body didn't produce eggs the way it should have for someone my age. This complication perplexed us, because the heavy amounts of medications being pumped in my body should have solved this issue. I had always thought if I had a diagnosis I would handle things better and then the doctors would know how to battle my issues. It didn't help at all.

The diagnosis only reminded me that my body continued to fail me, which sometimes brought ugly emotions and evil thoughts to the surface. "Teenage pregnancies? You have to be kidding me! Why, Lord? Pregnant drug addicts? Why, Lord?" I had to keep repeating the prayers I felt so deeply and reciting Joshua 1:9. I needed constant reminders that He was in control, and that I wanted what He wanted. If I wanted that mindset, I needed to continually practice it and repeat it out loud – His will, not mine. His will, not mine.

Have I not commanded you? Be strong and of good courage; do not be afraid, nor be dismayed, for the Lord your God is with you wherever you go. (Joshua 1:9)

When I decided to undergo IVF, I made the mistake of underestimating the complications involved in the treatment. Caught in the physical and emotional intensity of IVF, I couldn't deny that I still wrestled with my desire to control. I think the saying is "old habits die hard." Yes, they most certainly do. I thought I had beaten all those old feelings. Once again, my need for control had become a sin in my life, because I had forgotten that it was God who did the work, and it was hindering my relationship with Him. Continually, I remembered my convictions, asked for forgiveness, and gave things over to God again. It was an everyday process.

The doctor suggested that we do what is called a flare cycle. Basically, you begin another IVF cycle right away to try to "wake up" the ovaries. But this proved to be even more depressing. Despite the huge amounts of medications, zero follicles on my ovaries were the right size to contain mature eggs. I could not believe it. We didn't even have the option of converting the cycle to an IUI because I had zero eggs. I cried, I yelled, I wallowed in self-pity. And then I prayed the prayer that was becoming infused in my being: "God, please make a way where there is no way."

At this time the doctor discussed with us the possibility of using donor eggs. I prayed about this, but was quickly aware it wasn't an option for me. I felt that adoption was a better solution than using someone else's eggs, yet I didn't have a peace about adopting either. It was such an agonizing time, full of decisions. I felt God urging me to persevere, yet every door had closed. Actually, the doors had slammed shut in our faces. Our insurance money was running out, and I was more and more riddled with anxiety. During this time I poured my heart out to God like never before, and He was not silent.

The Lord put Psalm 91 on my heart. A side note in my Bible, dated 2-18-08, says, "I will continue to hold onto His promises. He is the deliverer, and victory only comes through Him! Praise the Lord my God forever! Amen."

I knew if I was going to survive this battle, then I had to have faith that He was and always would be the deliverer, and that He would most certainly deliver me. It did not necessarily mean I would get what I wanted, but I would receive exactly what He wanted for me. Intellectually, I know His will is always better than my own, but this godly principle practically had to be beaten into me. I had to die to what I wanted in order to recognize His will was optimal for my life. It wasn't getting any easier, but I knew it would ultimately become my saving grace.

It was around this time when I asked my doctor to please treat me for one more IVF cycle. I explained our insurance money was dwindling and this would be our last try regardless of the outcome. She was not at all positive and believed, based on what she had already seen medically, that the results of another cycle would probably prove to be negative. Reluctantly, she agreed to try one more time – as long as I recognized the odds were not favorable.

I believe all things are possible with God. I know He can move any mountain. My God is the God of miracles! He makes the crooked ways straight! And so I continued my prayer, "God, please make a way where there is no way."

When we first made the decision to seek treatment, we kept it very quiet. I felt a bit embarrassed by the circumstances of my infertility and inability to carry another baby to term. I don't know why I felt that way. Infertility is nothing to be embarrassed about. I could not change anything that had happened, and I did not ask for any of this to befall me. I felt convicted about feeling this way as we were ready to start our third cycle, so we started telling our parents, family, and wise Christian people who would pray for us. Prayer is a weapon against the enemy. My husband Paul and I needed it now more than ever. I was led to let others in on our journey after reading Matthew 15:28

> Then Jesus answered and said to her, "O woman, great is your faith! Let it be to you as you desire." And her daughter was healed from that very hour.
> (Matthew 15:28)

This passage refers to the mother of a demon possessed girl. She had such faith! She trusted Jesus could and would heal her daughter. Good parents who love their children want what is best for them. More importantly, parents who have a relationship with the Lord want God's will for their child's life. I encourage you to let your parents in on your journey and allow them to pray for you and carry some of your burden.

If you do not have the relationship you need for prayer support from your parents, I encourage you to find spiritual parents. A strong support system of older, wiser, caring people will love you, have faith enough to believe for you, and pray God's will in your life. You need a tremendous amount of support right now. Please do not shut yourself off because of humiliation, or because you feel that your situation might be a burden to someone else. I learned very quickly that it is essential to have someone wise in the ways of the Lord to lift you up in prayer. Encouragement is critical.

And Joses who was also named Barnabas
by the apostles (which is translated son of
encouragement), a Levite of the country of
Cyprus. (Acts 4:36)

Who is your encourager? We learn in the scriptures of
Barnabas, who was an encouragement to the apostle Paul. His
name even means "son of encouragement." This is no
coincidence. God sent Paul an encourager. Everyone needs
someone in her life to encourage her spiritually. If you do not
have someone to help build you up when you are feeling
helpless, it becomes easy to lose stamina on the journey. It is
very important to have at least one specific person in life who
can be your "cheerleader," someone you can confide in,
someone who will be a great source of encouragement to you.
This person can be your husband, sister, brother, or friend. I
am absolutely sure that God has sent you a Barnabas, and God
will use him or her to stand in the gap, if you will let Him.

The third and final cycle of IVF started just like the
other two. My hormone levels remained incredibly low. After
making some adjustments to my medications, we finally saw a
slow rise in my levels accompanied by a slow growth to the
follicles on my ovaries.

....

I encourage you to become your own medical advocate. Do not just trust what the physicians tell you. Instead, pray about it and do your own research. After a lot of studying, I realized my body was having an adverse reaction to one of the medications, so I contacted the doctor and we changed my meds. God gives us wisdom when we seek Him diligently. Don't be afraid to seek Him and research things yourself. He will open your eyes and show you if you allow Him.

Even with the slow rise in my hormone levels, we had little hope of finding any eggs in the follicles on my ovaries. Again, my doctor tried to persuade me to cancel the cycle and convert to an IUI, but I begged and pleaded and tried with everything in me to convey this was our last opportunity to conceive via assisted reproductive health care. I was willing to endure the egg retrieval surgery even if we were to find no eggs in the follicles. The doctor told me she would only perform the surgery if my numbers would rise significantly overnight. But until my lab results were confirmed, she refused to schedule the egg retrieval.

The next day I went for blood work. Later that afternoon I received a call that my numbers had jumped by more than one hundred points. My doctor was willing to schedule the surgery and we continued praying for a miracle.

At this point in a cycle, most people, especially when taking the amount of drugs I was taking, would have hormone levels in the thousands. Mine were still only in the low hundreds. The prayer was the same: "God, please make a way where there is no way."

At the egg retrieval a few days later, the doctor warned me again that I might not have any eggs in the four follicles on my ovaries. To further complicate things, the biggest and best looking follicle was on my right ovary, which she couldn't reach because of its position. We only had the left ovary, with three smaller follicles.

After her explanation, I was put to sleep while she performed the surgery. When I woke up from the anesthesia, I was thrilled to find out that she retrieved all three eggs from the follicles! The follicles weren't empty! That alone was a huge miracle. The next step was to use a procedure called icsi, in which the embryologist uses a needle and injects the egg with the sperm and waits to see if fertilization will take place.

The following day, a nurse called me to explain that one of the eggs retrieved was not mature and therefore was not useable, but that the other two did fertilize and were growing at the expected rate.

A few days later we had an eight cell embryo and a four cell embryo. I then underwent an embryo transfer, a procedure to place the embryos back in the uterus. I was sent home to rest... and wait.

We had to wait twelve days for the results from the blood pregnancy test. This was a very long twelve days, and like I've said before, patience has never ever, ever, ever been a virtue of mine.

After the first week, I took about ten pregnancy tests (literally!), even though this is something physicians advise you not to do. Before the retrieval surgery you are given a shot of HCG to make the eggs easier to retrieve. HCG is the hormone the body naturally makes when pregnant. If the HCG is still in your system from the injection, it can result in a false positive on a home pregnancy test. But since patience is not my virtue, punctuated by the fact my husband was on a business trip and not around to discourage me from taking the tests, I took them anyway. Every single one of them was positive, and every day I took a new one, I watched the test lines grow darker and darker pink, which was a sign that my body was making new HCG from a pregnancy.

You would expect that I would have been jumping up and down from witnessing two pink lines. I had doubted this day would ever come again. I called my friend, desperately crying my eyes out to tell her what I had done, and that the result was positive. She asked, "Isn't this what we're aiming for?" I was so emotional that I couldn't exactly comprehend what was happening. I refused to believe the home tests until I had confirmation from the blood pregnancy test.

I was a nervous wreck when I went in for the blood test, and when I returned home from the appointment, I literally sat on my bed all day staring at the phone just waiting for it to ring. After what seemed an eternity, the phone finally did ring and the results were indeed positive. I was pregnant!

20

Eighth Pregnancy:

Pursuing the Victor

May He send you help from the sanctuary,
and strengthen you out of Zion.
(Psalm 20:2)

This chapter is a psalm of David. Many of David's psalms are his cry for God to deliver him, protect him, and take down his enemies. The great stress and strain of battle led mighty King David before the throne of God the Almighty, where he asked the Lord for His valiant helping hand to ensure victory. In time of war, these pleas must have been the only thing that would bring peace to his heart. When we want victory, we must pursue the Victor.

We struggled immensely before we decided to turn to IVF. Questions of morality plagued my mind, and I wondered whether, if God wanted me to have another baby, I would have become pregnant on my own. Why should I have had to go to extreme measures? Maybe I was trying to break down a door with a deadbolt that God had installed, and I was meant to leave it alone. Even so, while I agonized over these decisions, I felt the still soft whisper in my heart from my Victor telling me to pursue my victory. Why did I have to go through IVF rather than just have Him open my womb "the old-fashioned way"? I don't know, but this was my battle and the way the Lord intended to teach me to walk and trust.

The following analogy might be a stretch, but indulge me as I feel it explains my point. When we have a cavity, I guess it's conceivable that God Himself could reach down in the middle of the night and fill our tooth, but He doesn't usually work that way. He sends help in the form of the dentist chair and drill that none of us wants to face. Throughout all I had endured, I knew that, regardless of the outcome, I was extremely blessed to have the privilege of pursuing the victor.

The first concern of a confirmed pregnancy achieved via IVF is that it may result in a tubal pregnancy. This happens when the embryos float around and settle in a fallopian tube rather than in the uterus after being injected back inside the body. Forty-eight hours after the original pregnancy test, a follow up blood pregnancy test is required, with the hope that HCG levels will double. If they do, the pregnancy is probably progressing normally. My numbers tripled! The next step was an ultrasound to make sure everything looked as it was supposed to and to see if one or both embryos implanted.

On the day of my ultrasound appointment, I was six weeks pregnant. The test seemed to take forever. Normally, my husband would come into the ultrasound room with me, but this time, they made him wait in the waiting room until the results were ready to be shown. The technician was watching the screen, measuring everything, careful not to allow me to see my part of the screen until she was finished

....

and able to explain everything. This was nerve wracking. I prayed and prayed while lying on the table, but anxiety was taking over. I had lived through so much disappointment up to this moment, and I was not sure if I would be able to handle bad news. My husband, who is always the calm one of the two of us, was just as anxious as I.

When she finally finished the test, she brought Paul back to join me. He came and took the seat next to me. We looked at each other, held hands tightly, and took a deep breath. At this time the tech turned the screen toward us and simply said, "Here is baby A and here is baby B." The first thing my husband said was, "I knew it!" I just cried.

After the ultrasound, we were taken back to a conference room where the doctor admitted she was shocked I was pregnant. She had never seen anyone with an E2 level as low as mine actually become pregnant. Then she blurted out the many frightening statistics concerning vanishing twin and so on, and warned us, "We are not out of the woods yet." She sent me home with a follow-up ultrasound appointment in two weeks which would determine how good things "really" looked. I tried hard not to look at what could go wrong and praised God for the miracle of that day. I was pregnant with twins!

My eight week ultrasound was as nerve wracking as the first. Already, I was so sick and vomiting so frequently that I had been in the emergency room on IV to control the dehydration. With my history, coupled with the fact that I had no bleeding, this was likely a sign that everything was okay. The ultrasound results were great; both babies were growing at the same rate and looking very healthy. I kept praying that God would make a way where there was no way, and so far, He was doing just that.

....

I then was released to my regular obstetrician for care, and boy, did I prove to need a lot of it. I took intramuscular shots of progesterone until we could hear a heartbeat (with twins you generally cannot hear both heartbeats until a little later in the pregnancy), so my appointments started earlier than normal. We were able to hear one heartbeat at a little over eight weeks; at that point I was able to discontinue the shots.

I continued to feel sicker than I ever had in all my life. Constantly, I was in and out of the hospital for dehydration. I could keep nothing down, and my electrolyte levels were off balance, which caused cramping. This is scary for anyone, even if you haven't endured miscarriages. I was admitted into the hospital for a few days to balance my electrolytes and to be re-hydrated. The doctors decided (with pressure from my husband) that I needed a pic line put in to keep my body from continual dehydration.

After I was discharged, the pic line was put in, and home nurses came to check my progress and make sure my line was clean. Although I still vomited often, I was not quite as sick because I was staying hydrated. Finally at eighteen weeks the vomiting relented, and by twenty-two weeks the pic line was removed. Although I was still nauseated most of the time, I was better able to control it. That's when I started having lots of pain in my legs that was so intense that I couldn't walk very well. I had to use a cane at home and a wheelchair outside the home.

My health was a bit out of control. I had pregnancy-induced carpal tunnel, pregnancy-induced eczema (I didn't even know such things existed), pregnancy-induced vomiting . . . I pretty much had pregnancy-induced everything. You name it – I had it! However, what mattered most to me was the health of the babies, and both were holding up beautifully.

....

The worst came when, at thirty-three weeks, I had protein in my urine and a spike in my blood pressure. By thirty-three weeks two days, I was admitted to the hospital with a diagnosis of pre-eclampsia. The doctors hoped that I would reach at least thirty-six weeks gestation, but this meant staying in the hospital for the duration of the pregnancy. Anything to protect the babies was fine with me.

On the day I was admitted to the hospital, the nurse administered my first steroid shot to help the babies' lungs mature. Twenty-four hours later I received another one. At thirty-three weeks six days, I woke up at two o'clock in the morning to what I thought was gas pain. I waited an hour before calling the nurse to tell her there was a possibility that I was experiencing contractions. The nurse brought in a monitor to check the babies. We needed to find out if what I was feeling was just my overindulgence of hospital food and take-out (since I had nothing to do but lie there and eat) or contractions.

It was contractions. I was having them every four minutes. They paged the resident on call to come check me and report to my doctor. I called my husband right away. He had been staying with me every night at the hospital, but since this was Saturday night, I had wanted him go home in hopes of finally having a good night's sleep in his own bed and taking our son to church the next morning. They both needed some normalcy. But this night turned out to be anything but normal. Of all nights to send him home!

The moment when Paul heard my voice on the telephone he wanted to rush to the hospital, but I told him to wait until we found out what the doctor thought. At that point I was one centimeter dilated and sixty percent effaced. The resident left to contact my doctor with a report of what was happening. While she was gone, the contractions grew stronger. Thirty minutes later, the resident returned and informed me that my doctor wanted her to examine me one more time before we made a decision on pain management. Only thirty minutes later, I was already three centimeters dilated and one hundred percent effaced. The resident, along with my doctor, made the decision to deliver the babies.

I called my husband, who woke up our son Pauly, raced to take him to my mother's house, and then headed to the hospital. As he tried to enter the parkway to head to the hospital, it was, of course, closed due to construction. At the rate Paul was going, it was going to take him more than twice the usual time to arrive at the hospital, which was already forty-five minutes away. While they were prepping me for surgery, I was a nervous wreck about Paul not being there.

I had to have a C-section because baby "A" was breech and baby "B" was transverse. It frightened me even more to see two teams from the neonatal intensive care unit already in the room: one for each baby. Looking at all the medical equipment had me feeling only panic and anxiety. I worried about how well the babies would be able to breathe on their own or how big they would be. Tiny intubation tubes are a scary sight for a mother about to deliver. No one knew how much medical intervention might be needed. I was screaming out in my mind, "God, make a way where there is no way!"

The anesthesiologist gave me a spinal block, and then at the last minute, Paul raced into the operating room with a very stylish pair of blue scrubs on, matching cap, face mask, and an undeniable nervous excitement that he just could not contain. This was what we had waited and prayed for all these years. It was finally harvest time.

A very short time later, baby "A," Samuel Ryan Kostick, was born. Three minutes later, baby "B," Grace Jane Kostick, followed. Samuel weighed 3 lbs. 14 oz. and Grace 3 lbs. 9 oz. Each was so tiny. The neonatal teams took them to the N.I.C.U. (Neonatal Intensive Care Unit) for testing and care while the doctors finished up my surgery.

The next few days, for me, are actually quite hazy. Due to the magnesium medication administered to treat the pre-eclampsia and all the other pain meds from the C-section, I was very sick. I even had a hard time traveling down to the N.I.C.U. to visit the babies. My husband was definitely a favorite of the nurses in the N.I.C.U. He spent most of his time those first few days learning how to take care of premature twins. He made sure my bed rails and the walls of my hospital room were covered with pictures of them.

Five days later, I was released, but both babies needed to stay in the N.I.C.U. This was very difficult for me. Several years earlier, I had left the hospital without my baby, and the reality of that dreadful situation was that I never had the opportunity to bring my baby girl home. No matter how hard I tried, I could not stop the flood of vivid images from that horrendous day. They invaded my every thought. The memories of leaving with empty arms and an empty heart began to override the elation of having newborn twins. The day I was sent home without my babies was probably the worst day of fear I had experienced since watching my baby daughter Courtney's pink casket being lowered into a grave. I knew in my heart that my babies would be okay, but I could not shake the questioning "what ifs" from my mind.

21

Victory in Jesus

The twins spent their days in the N.I.C.U. growing and being observed to make sure they were well enough to go home. I thank God that neither child needed any breathing tubes or serious medical intervention. Both ended up being completely healthy, and I did bring both of my babies home! I know that my God is the God of miracles; I have seen them with my own eyes. In fact, my little miracles are giggling and smiling right now as I am stealing this quick moment to write.

> But those who wait on the Lord shall
> renew their strength; they shall mount up
> with wings like eagles, they shall run and
> not be weary, they shall walk and not faint.
> (Isaiah 40:31)

It is entirely too easy to become weary while waiting. I waited for more than fifteen years for God to answer my

....

prayer. Regardless of whether I wanted to be patient, I had to be. Though it was hard to see at the time, when I look back, I can see God's fingerprints all over my circumstances. From my darkest day to the day I was delivered, He was there. I may not have always felt it, but He did renew my strength.

When Samuel and Grace came home, we started a new life together – my husband, me, and our *three* kids! I now have the family that I had always dreamed about. God delivered us from fifteen years of hurting and pain. The losses of the six other babies will never be forgotten and the pain will never fully leave, but joy came in the morning, through the mourning. God made a way where there was no way!

I am forever changed by all the circumstances of the last several years of my life. Yes, I still fight some fear and anxiety, but I know how to fight those and will gladly war against them in recognition of the greatness of my God. I am learning daily that, just because new problems and issues arise in my life, I do not want what I call "transference of burdens" – I do not want to give one burden to Jesus just to carry another. I cannot pick and choose which burdens to give Him, as if I can handle some on my own. I'm learning to begin each day by giving the Lord new burdens and worries that arise in my life, and to use lessons learned throughout my previous struggles to maintain victory in every area. Through this process, I am being transformed and molded into a new person, and, hopefully, every day I am becoming more like the person God intends for me to be.

....

Life is hectic now. As I sit here writing, I have two beautiful five-year-old children, joyfully chasing each other around, and a twenty-one year old young man who is beginning to make his own mark on the world. All three are miracles. After all the years gone by, and all the soul searching, I've realized that each baby who was placed in my womb was a miracle. They were incredible gifts of life from the Creator who thought enough of me to breathe life inside my body. Whether I was able to keep that life or not, each child was mine, and I loved them all. Throughout fifteen years of adversity, God has shown me His great love. I've received His mercy in the face of unfathomable sorrow.

Now that I have experienced such goodness in my life, I cannot help but wonder about the lives of the people around me. I wonder what it is that God has planned for them. I wonder how many miracles we experience on a daily basis that we do not even recognize as such. If we allow Him, He will work in us. I take great comfort in the fact that He is always working for us. Romans 8:31 points out that if God is for us, who can be against us?

Regardless of how you feel on any given day, just remember that God is for you! There were many times I felt the whole world caving in around me. I found it hard to believe anyone could understand my pain. I remember one instance, when an old acquaintance I had not seen in a few years spotted me in a crowd. She approached me and asked, "Did you ever have a baby?" I remember feeling such shame in my answer, which was, of course, "No."

I allowed myself to feel shame over a situation I could not control and did not ask for. I felt attacked on every front. Still, although I lost some battles, I eventually won the war. This was not just because I was blessed with more children, but because I slowly but surely allowed God to work in my life. I took a stand against feeling shame and found my security in Him. He is always working for us; we are His children.

> But as many as received Him, to them He gave the right to become children of God, to those who believe in His name: who were born, not of blood, nor of the will of the flesh, nor of the will of man, but of God. (John 1:12-13)

In conclusion, if you have not yet made a personal commitment to serve Jesus Christ and make Him Lord of your life, then I ask you to ponder these two scriptures. By asking Him into our hearts and lives, we become His children. Please understand that, without Him, I would have been completely lost in a sea of doubt. I want to make it very clear that I never would have made it through the fire without a personal relationship with the Lord. I am His child; I believe in His name. Without Him, hope does not come easily – in fact, it may never come at all. He is our hope.

Those of us who already have a personal relationship with Christ still struggle when times are tough. I never would have found peace after such loss, had I not surrendered my life to Jesus.

There are no rituals to follow when asking Jesus into your heart and life. You can pray alone or with someone else. Today is a new day. Cling to Him and whisper those life-

....

changing words: "Lord, forgive me of my sins, come into my life, and change my heart. I believe in You; I want to know You. I am Yours."

Through the Lord's mercies we are not consumed, because His compassions fail not. They are new every morning; great is Your faithfulness. (Lamentations 3:22-23)

I hope my story has helped plant seeds of hope, faith, and encouragement for you. May God continue to work in your life through your circumstances, and may you reach out and take hold of the hem of His garment. God is faithful!

O Lord, You are my God. I will exalt You, I will praise Your name, for You have done wonderful things; Your counsels of old are faithfulness and truth. (Isaiah 25:1)

Praising Him through the storms of life is essential. There is no alternative. I spoke in my testimony of experiencing miracles one step at a time. Sometimes we are totally unaware of these miracles. It is possible that you and I both may be experiencing one today. Let's praise Him for miracles that are acquired in small steps. Let us be content with the knowledge that He is faithful. His counsels of old are faithfulness and truth. How many people in the world do we encounter with such attributes? None is as faithful as He. He is wonderful, and He has done wonderful things. Exalt Him today.

When you have nothing left to hold, you can always hold hope.

Acknowledgments

To my Lord and Savior Jesus Christ: It is amazing to me how You have turned my scars into lines of a story meant to shout praise unto Your mighty name. You are far more faithful than I deserve, and I love You with my whole heart. I only have worth because You are worthy.

Paul: I still cannot believe how God designed our two lives to meet so young, and complement each other so beautifully to work together to further the kingdom of Christ. You are my biggest fan and sweetest treasure. Thank you for always putting Christ first so that you can continue to pour out love to us and so many who need you. You are my life, and each moment together is a gift. I love you!

Patty Buirge: Thank you for working tirelessly on the first edits of this book. You were an answer to prayer in a time of need.

Emily Wood: Thank you for the gentle ways you guide me as you edit my work. Your gifts do not go unnoticed, and I cannot wait to read one of your books one day! May God continue to use your offerings to bring Him glory. Thank you, my friend!

....

Kathy Inocelda: Thank you for being the friend I needed to get through the hardest moments of my life. I will never forget your weary head on the side of my hospital bed praying that I would be okay. You were heaven sent, and I love you!

Star Laliberte: Thank you for every prayer, every trip to the hospital, and every injection administered when Paul was out of town. You always go far above and beyond what I need when I need it. You are precious to me.

To the Maust family: I would have never made it through the creative process of this book without ALL of you. Thanks for everything.

To every friend who has ever come alongside me in prayer: Thank you for the meals you made when I was sicker than sick. I covet each of you. This little book would turn into a novel if I mentioned all of you. You know who you are, and I adore every one of you!

To my parents: Thank you for all your prayers and support. I am truly blessed to have so much love in my life.

To my family: You cried with me and hoped against all odds that things would turn around. You beat God's ear, and there will never be words to thank you enough!

To Pauly, Samuel, and Grace: You three are miracles and daily reminders of God's faithfulness and deep love for me. Always, always, always serve Him. Nothing will ever be more important in your lives than your relationship with the living God. Through the darkest times He will be your Light. I promise.

To the five babies I never held: The hands you find yourselves in are so much better than the human hands who type these words. I will always miss you and wonder who you might have been, but I know someday our reunion will be the sweetest of all time. Your mama loves you so much!

To Courtney: Almost eighteen years later you still run through my dreams. I envision your smile and hair color. I see your eyes all lit up with the light of Jesus, and I envy the Hands that hold you tight. I long to be with you but know this life will move quickly and my purpose was meant to be far different than yours. You are forever my daughter, and I can't wait to hold you again. Give my Jesus a big hug for me, and tell Him thank You for His faithfulness and love. You've been gifted eternal joy, never to know the stains and sorrow of this world. You are blessed, my little one.

About Jennifer

Jennifer Kostick - has been married for twenty-two years to her high school sweetheart, Paul. She is a speaker, blogger, and the founder of A Girl on the Doorstep Ministries.

Jennifer blogs at www.agirlonthedoorstep.com where she passionately encourages women through a godly message of mercy and hope.

Connect with Jennifer

AGirlontheDoorstep.com

Twitter.com/GirlonDoorstep

Facebook.com/agirlonthedoorstep

JenniferKostick.com

You can connect with

Jennifer

on her blog

AGirlontheDoorstep.com

 AGirlontheDoorstep

 @GirlonDoorstep